awfully hilarious

Stories we Never Tell

Imagined by

Heather Hendrie

ISBN 978-1-7388035-0-7
Printed and bound worldwide by Amazon

Editing thanks to
Meg Power of Squamish, BC
Translations
by Pierre-Olivier Gaudreault of Squamish, BC
Design, layout, and cover design
by Ken Braithwaite
Proof reading thanks to
Anne Hendrie, and Pamela Murchison
Moon Illustrations courtesy of
Minimal Souls Studio.

In dedication to love,
in all its forms.

"When we love,
we can let our hearts speak."

~bell hooks. all about love.

Maybe the journey
isn't so much about
becoming anything.

Maybe it's about
un-becoming everything
that isn't really you,
so you can be who
you were meant to be
in the first place.

~Paulo Coelho

(you're so) Foreword

(Yeah, yeah, I get that a lot).

Welcome, we're so glad you're here!

We are grateful to whatever or whomever has brought you here, whether that be a yeast infection that just wouldn't quit, a terrible Tinder date, or just plain curiosity. We'll begin with what this isn't: it's not a roast, it isn't to poke fun, it isn't to hurt anyone. All stories here have been written with love and a compassionate eye for personal growth on the part of the writer. Names, and any identifying details, in stories have been changed so as to protect anyone who may not have chosen to be featured on these pages. We're here to bring levity, laughter, and support for one another by sharing some deeply personal stories, again, not to point fingers at individuals, but to shine a spotlight on the larger systems at play that cause us to feel so alone in the times when we need one another most.

This project came about, as so many do, when I was focusing on something else entirely. I was writing a book about trying to ride the waves of cyclical hormones against the current of a linear society (see what I did there? #shamelessselfpromo) when I went on a truly bad date that diverted my focus. I cried after first meeting Parachute Boy, but afterwards, in sharing the story with friends, I laughed so hard I snorted the juice I was drinking out of my nostrils and, as so often happens with stories, once I shared mine, others had tales to tell too. We started around the kitchen table, a group of roommates who'd all lived on 5A Street in Calgary, and then the tales took on a life of their own, travelling rapidly beyond those borders.

Folks who brought their stories to the table chose to be here, and of course there are others who were invited and weren't yet ready to share; meaning, some voices are notably absent, and so you may notice some that are missing, or that these stories may be derived from one particular perspective or another. What we hope you will find on these pages is personal experience, an attempt to process pain, to understand ourselves better and to reclaim ourselves in the retelling (I mean, it would be awesome to transform unhelpful and damaging societal structures—#fuckthepatriarchy—but for now we're winning if we make you laugh, if we make you feel, if we make you feel any less alone). And if you've got a story of your own to share (I know you do!), reach out anytime—hallllloooooooo sequel!

We're here to laugh together about those things that can often leave us feeling awful and alone. This publication, *the awfully hilarious project*, arose to transmute those true and taboo or traumatic incidents that are just so awful alone, into something just a little bit more hilarious. May this space allow us to come together to grieve the losses and misfortunes of dating, love, or (Goddess-forbid) menstruating or performing a bodily function under the umbrella of our current patriarchal frame. Shit the bed in Machu Picchu? Been there, done that. Peed your pants on a first date? Check. Landed in the ER after a thwarted attempt at self-healing with a garlic clove? We've got you. We feel you. What you'll find are some hard, heart-opening stories to remind you that maybe we're all just a little bit lost together on this journey towards freedom, truth, ecstasy, love, and growing the fuck up in a society that would push us otherwise.

The sequence of events on these pages are non-sequential and non-linear (because we've seen what straight lines and box-shaped structures can do to a person, and hey, life just isn't linear, is it?). As the world turns, the flow of our stories follow the phases of the moon, as experiences wax and wane, we complete a cycle and become full and then a new cycle begins.

We're delighted to have you here with us as we create, grieve, celebrate, and talk openly about those things that culture has made taboo, while laughing our asses off, of course.

So, cheers!
Love,

Heather & all of us here at
the awfully hilarious project

Seasons of the Moon

Winter Moons

Spring Moons

Summer Moons

Fall Moons

Winter Moons

Vodka, Straight

Sarah Richards Graba

I'm going to share with you the story about the first time I got really drunk.

Now, this wasn't the first time I'd had alcohol; I had been to house parties with beer and hard liquor, or wine spritzers and malted drinks. I'd had wine with my parents on holidays and special occasions. It also wasn't the first time I had felt the effects of alcohol; I had been buzzed before. But this night was the first time I got really, really drunk—throw-up drunk. Hangover drunk.

And that's because I had six shots of vodka in two hours.

I was 17, a senior in high school. My friends picked me up to go hang out with some frat guys in the nearby college town of Boulder, Colorado.

We went to the University of Colorado (CU) campus to meet up with some guy my friend Brianna knew and hang out at his dorm room. I don't actually remember how Brianna knew him —it seemed like she was always meeting random guys at clubs (on under-18 nights) or at house parties. But there we were, in a tiny garden-level dorm room—three guys, my two friends, me, and a bottle of vodka. No mixers, just straight vodka.

I don't remember what we were doing, besides just drinking, maybe some talking. I'm sure there was flirting going on (my friends and I were always on the prowl for fun new boys), but I don't remember if there was anything on TV, or if there was music playing. I only remember that I got very drunk very fast.

Brianna, who was the designated driver, drove me home. She had red hair and freckles and the most amazing rack. She was my troublemaker friend, the one who challenged me to push boundaries. My other friend, Andrea, who I'd known since elementary school (and was slightly more practical, but easily influenced by Brianna), stopped me for a moment and asked, "Are you ok?" as they dropped me off. I told them I was fine. It was about 10 or 11pm at night—not super late or anything, and I wasn't out past curfew.

I walked in the house and upstairs, to my bedroom. My bedroom was right across from my parents. My brother and my parents were already upstairs and in their rooms for the night. The lights were off. I prayed that everyone was asleep, and I could make it to my room undetected.

No such luck. When I reached the landing, I heard my mom's voice from the open door to her bedroom on my right: "Sarah—come here."

My mom is Korean, and there's a very specific Korean way she says my name when I'm in trouble. It's deep, staccato. Choppy, like the Korean language. Blocks of syllables. SAE-RAH. COME. HERE.

I stood in the doorway, hoping that the distance and darkness would mask my intoxication. "Hi Mom. I'm home—I'm just going to bed."

"Come here."

I stepped into her dark room and stood at her bedside, near her feet.

"Closer."

I knelt next to her.

"You are drunk."

"I had a little wine," I said, trying not to breathe too heavily for fear of the alcohol on my breath. "It's fine, Brianna drove, and she didn't have anything."

"You are drunk."

I don't remember the entire conversation clearly, but I recall I was giggling a little. Like I couldn't help myself. Knowing that I was caught, but all I could do was giggle at the situation.

"Go to bed," my mom said, disgusted with me.

"That's where I was going," I replied.

I was ready to pass out and went to sleep easily. A few hours later, I woke up sick to my stomach. I rushed to the bathroom and began vomiting.

My parents woke up, of course. My mom stood in the doorway to the bathroom, arms crossed, so angry, unable to say anything.

My dad, a white guy from Texas, was laughing his ass off.

"You're praying to the porcelain god now, aren't you?" he chortled. He took delight in my suffering, but I wasn't angry at him. I preferred his teasing to my mom's quiet, seething anger. My mom almost couldn't look at me.

By the time I finished puking, I wanted to just lie down and go to sleep. My dad stayed in my room with me; my mom was unable to be in my presence any longer.

I remember lying in bed, crying. "I'm so tired, Dad! But the room won't stop spinning.

"Put your foot on the floor," he said. "That works every time."

I snaked one bare foot out from under the covers and placed the sole of my foot flat against the floor. Immediately the room righted itself. It was still swimming a little, still watery, but the uncontrollable spinning had stopped. I finally went back to sleep, but never forgot that trick. I use it to this day if I've had too much to drink.

The next morning, over my awful hangover, I got an earful from my mom about responsibility (and my lack of it), about the harm I did to my body, about safety, etc. She grounded me until I turned 18. Luckily, I was only a month and a half away from my birthday but still, it was the longest I had ever been grounded before. It was also the last time my mom ever grounded me. I moved out of the house a few months later and into a dorm room at CU.

Now that I'm a grown woman with a daughter of my own, I think back to how dangerous it was for me and my friends to get drunk so quickly with boys who we didn't know. I was lucky that I just got away with an awful night of vomiting, a dreadful hangover, and punishment from my parents. However, learning to stick my foot on the ground to right myself when the world is spinning—that was a lesson that I've applied beyond drunken foolishness. After oceans of vomit, my dad had given me a little buried treasure—a nugget of golden wisdom.

Vodka, funnily enough, continues to be one of my liquors of choice. But vodka straight has definitely lost its appeal.

B

Texting is the worst

The first time I met Aaron, I could not believe this was a real person

I was staring at a closed gate and his first words to me were, "Can I give you a boost?"

Those are the best words I could hope to hear at a locked gate, and I was immediately smitten.

He would hold out his hand every time we walked on ice ... just in case I slipped

He was gracious, he was kind, and he climbed!

He had a consistency in texting that I could not compete with

There were great baking and cooking sessions

Conversations on the couch where we opened our hearts

Chatted about how we felt about kids,
getting older,

But then he got busy, and the texts dwindled

I enquired first, asked if I could help

Down to one sentence texts

Then I called him out on it

No more texts.

B

Texting is the worst (reprise)

The worst sound when being ghosted
Is the sound of an incoming text
Your heart, despite repeated reprimands
Does a little leap
Maybe this time?
You admonish yourself
Remind yourself this is not going to happen
But that stupid little heart that has no braincells
(how come evolution didn't favour that?)
Just relentlessly continues to leap
And after the split second it takes to confirm
what you already knew
It dives into despair
Yeah mom, dad, sis, sarah, I love you guyses
But right now, seeing your name only causes
me pain

The Garlic Clove

Alternate title: A Case for Canesten

Heather Hendrie

I felt a pinch in my ovary on the day my nephew Charlie was born to my younger sister Martha, making me an aunt for the first time. I have now, twice over, become a sister-in-law to my younger sisters' husbands, and have the great joy of my five nieces, but Charlie was my first nephew.

I wasn't present when he arrived. I wish I'd been there to hold my sister's hand and to look into his eyes the moment they first opened onto the world. But no, I was away on Vancouver Island, and I think Martha was in labour at the exact moment that I keeled over in the ditch.
Picture this now for a moment: a blissful scene as I run along a tree-lined dirt road, dappled with summer sunspots just like me. Beautiful

thimbleberries and salmonberries in their spectrum of oranges and reds are ripening along the roadside and everything smells like summer. A gentle breeze plays with my curls as I jog—and then I fall over. What seems like a while later, I find myself prostrate with the forget-me-nots in the trash and gravel of the ditch. A sticky Oh Henry! wrapper sticks to my calf as I curl up in pain, feeling an intense burning rising from somewhere near my left ovary. Rivulets of sweat stream salt into my eyes and I struggle to stay conscious.

That's when it comes to me, "Dammit! There's a clove of garlic up there."

If you could imagine for a moment touching freshly minced garlic to your eyeball, multiply the sensation by 100, insert the smell of trash and fresh dog poo and you'll be about ready to join me in the ditch.

I could start to spin out on the Patriarchy and why the supposed secrecy of anything to do with my vagina, periods, hormones, or sexuality are really why I've landed in the ditch, but I'll leave that for a little later and for now we'll stick to the specifics of this particular situation.

I had tried to extract the offending clove two days ago in an intense bathroom stall yoga session. Panting and frustrated, I'd given up in vain, hoping it would eventually just work itself out. Like so many other pain points, clearly, it hadn't.

I was at a summer camp for adults, training with a woman named Joanna Macy in my most recent passion, Ecopsychology. Tucked away on Vancouver Island, we slept in cabins on a gorgeous inlet of the Pacific Ocean. Eagles flew overhead, and otters played in the waves. It was idyllic, except for this one thing.

I had really hoped the whole situation would either just resolve itself or wait until my eventual return to civilization. How, you may be wondering, did I get myself into this pickle? It was the result of necessity. Necessity as they say, is the mother of invention (and the occasionally disastrous idea). It started a week ago. Three days into the camp I noticed that it was getting itchy down there. I mean, *really* itchy. As in mosquito bite in my crotch, resulting in a burning need to surreptitiously scratch it on coffee breaks and shuffle just a little too much in my seat kind of itchy. Of course, I recognized the feeling. I'd known it before, after each new lover, a course of antibiotics, or just a few days after Halloween and all those mini chocolate bars. I could usually solve it all very easily with a quick trip to the drug store (except in Latin America, but that's another story. Who knew that my loose translation of *vaginal mushroom* would not get me what I needed in a Peruvian pharmacy?)

So, stuck here, 30 minutes by car from the nearest drugstore, I asked my campmates if anyone had brought any anti-fungal cream with them. Not surprisingly (think hippie summer camp for adults) nobody had brought anything remotely resembling a pharmaceutical drug (Goddess-forbid!). That's when Tree, a short-haired pixie in flowing pants suggested, "Why not try yoghurt?"

"Or a garlic clove? That always works for me," chimed Leila from the top bunk.

They didn't describe the treatments in any further detail. I didn't ask for more either, because these kinds of topics have always felt so awkward to me.

I ignored the girls' advice for a little while but two days later, now desperate, I snuck a little bowl of yoghurt away from the breakfast buffet. It was awkward to veil it with my tank top as I snuck away into the bathroom and even more uncomfortable to waddle back out again after spooning the gloopy, white, live-culture over my nether-regions.

The slimy intervention came with numerous side-effects, the least of which was the white goop that coolly rode down my left thigh, stopped short at my sock and then slid off onto the floor during a moment when I hoped no one was watching.

And so, there I was two days later, surreptitiously asking the kitchen staff for some garlic. They gave me two cloves. These were at least easier to tuck into my pocket as I made my way to the bathroom. Gritting my teeth, I inserted the savoury suppository and exhaled deeply.

"This better fucking work," I muttered under my breath.

But as you can so clearly see, it didn't.

So now, I'm lying in the ditch, where we first started this story, sweating and pinpointing the exact source of my problem to that clove-shaped bit of fire next to my uterus. I take a deep breath in, prop myself up on my elbows and slowly limp home.

An hour later I'm drenched in sweat and back in our dorm room. I pause to stick my head under the sink, grateful for the cold water running down the back of my neck, then make a beeline for the one woman there with a car.

"Tree," I ask weakly, "Could you please take me to the hospital?"

En route she went into a very uncompassionate lecture about how I should have put the garlic clove into a stocking prior to insertion to facilitate extraction. For one thing, that would have been good to know four days ago, but on the other hand, I'd never have had the necessary tools because stockings are but one aspect of society's grooming of me to be a "good woman" I'd had the good sense to find so constraining, that I had ditched them completely by the age of four. I wish I had the good sense to do the same with the rest of it as I lay thrashing about on the kitchen floor in my leotards, deliberately ripping an enormous hole through the crotch of the offending garment, thereby achieving the excellent multi-pronged win of never having to wear them again, nor having to attend Sunday school that morning. (The joy that came from that early win is likely what led me to become a revolutionary, I expect.)

Only now, at the age of 43, and diagnosed with a chronic health condition that much of "the establishment" barely considers valid (yet valid enough that I've been declined disability coverage by the insurance companies for my atypical response to the hormone progesterone) have I begun to realise the extent to which people must go to receive care. Women's health has been made secret and shameful for so long, we tend not to question it. But as I grow older and wiser, I'm done with the backroom cures. It's time to bring it all to the fore. Back then though, I was still shy about it as I shamefacedly approached the triage desk in Victoria's Emergency Room.

"Umm...I'm really sorry, I'm kind of embarrassed. I hate to be a drain on the system, but...well...I have a yeast infection and I tried to take care of it myself, and..."
I didn't get to the part about what I'd done to treat myself before the nurse in this progressive city full of hippies interrupted me, shook her head, and rolled her eyes, "My god honey, this is Victoria, British Columbia. You think we don't see this every day? I recommend you girls give Western medicine a try sometime. Take a seat, and we'll get to that garlic clove as soon as there's an opening."

(And do you know, the nurse who treated me had the audacity, or maybe the generosity, to offer me back the offending spice following the extraction!)

I'm pleased to report that I healed quickly after the procedure and left the clove and its proponents behind on Vancouver Island. It wasn't the first or the last time that I would listen to someone else's advice over my own gut knowledge of what works for me, but we'll talk more about that later when it comes to dating, oral contraceptives, and my career.

After the ordeal I flew home, where I met and held my dear nephew Charlie for the first time. His skin felt like velvet against my hand, and I got to bathe him with my mother in the kitchen sink. Seeing my sister become a mother and meeting this beautiful baby boy was the very start of me beginning to slowly shift the way I see, understand, and relate not only to men, but to myself as a woman. In essence: to everyone simply as humans, trying our very best. But again, more on that later.

Sophie Balisky

Ophelia Survives

I once wrapped romantic
Around my body like a black lace dress
Weighed down, neck deep
In the doldrums of another's despair
The flowers in my hair floated away like flotsam
Perpetually patient for promised potential
Until the darkness of a lover
Decomposed my colour.

I had to tear myself free from the hopeless, heavy fabric
Of a fairy tale illusion
Abandon the fabrication of my ability
To save those already lost to the current
I coughed the dead-water from my lungs

As I dragged my body back to shore.
I've wrung my heart out on these banks
Fashioned effigies of my own undoings
I burn past versions of myself like incense
Adorn my brow with forget-me-nots
And rosemary to remember
That I deserve to feel the sun
Bare feet stand on solid ground
The days I drown for love are done.

A Hard Pill to Swallow, But Not as Hard as I Thought

Kate van Fraassen

We were only a few months into our relationship, I was living in a small mountain town, and he was living in the city. I sat, stressing out in the desperately-needing-to-be-renovated bathroom of his older house in a quirky inner-city neighbourhood. I was regularly going through the existential crisis of imagining myself living in the city again. Would I lose my love for adventure? Would I still be able to identify as an "outdoorsy" person if I lived amongst high-rises and traffic jams? Do I want to give up my mountain lifestyle for a guy?! Would I really be giving anything up, or adding something deeper to my life? Will this bathroom ever get updated? But none of that mattered now. I was fumbling with a box that contained a cure for my current vulva-related emergency.

It wasn't anything serious. Just a yeast infection. The emergency was that it was interrupting my ability to enjoy a lustful moment with a guy I was starting to really fall for. I was visiting for the weekend and didn't have the patience for bodily challenges to stand in the way of having great sex. At the time I was all about taking a more natural approach to my health, but I needed to get things calmed down fast. I didn't have time to wait for my body to work out its own pH balance.

I finally got the package open and paused for a nano-second at the size of the pill, but due to my libido-fueled rush to get out of the bathroom and back into bed, I popped the pill in my mouth, took a big swig of water, and tried to swallow. It took a moment. The pill seemed oddly large as I waited for it to make its way down my throat. Suddenly I had a moment of panic. Fuck! Was that an oral pill? Or a vaginal pill!? I grabbed the box from the garbage and read the package to confirm. "Oh fuck. Oh fuck, fuck!" I whispered to myself. I must have grabbed the suppository option by mistake.
Fuuuuuuuck! I stared at myself in the mirror. What do I do now?

Nothing kills the mood like swallowing a suppository. Blushing like I hadn't since junior high, I came out of the bathroom and back to the bed. I didn't know what to say. A year earlier I probably would have told some kind of feeble white lie about what had taken me so long in the bathroom. I would've swallowed any worry about having just ingested a suppository and carried on.

But I wasn't the woman I was a year ago. Slowly through reflection and evaluation of past experiences I had begun to unpack what mattered to me, not only in relationships, but in order to lay a foundation for intimacy: honesty, and openness being two key components. So, the new me swallowed my pride and told him what had just gone down.

"Oh no!" He looked at me trying not to laugh.

But he couldn't help it and pretty soon we were both laughing. My cheeks cooled down a little, my heart rate slowed, and the laughter subsided. We decided that we should probably call HealthLink to make sure everything was going to be okay.

Our relationship had started slowly, I think the deepening attraction and compatibility surprised us both. It wasn't all physical, but that part was great. This outdoorsy hippie girl was having conversations about things like genital health with a mountain bike dude (what!?). It was taking time for me to settle into being comfortable and confident talking about vulnerable topics with a guy. But the willingness of both of us to wade through those awkward conversations set us up for this one.

The HealthLink nurse was helpful and assured me that despite ingesting the pill, all was well and it should still be able to do its thing, which was reassuring, despite the embarrassment of my mistake.

Perhaps the most reassuring was that the night wasn't ruined. We were able to laugh at the awkwardness of it all and put aside my discomfort in talking about things like yeast infections, which made it easier for me to put aside my embarrassment about my vulvar health, not to mention my embarrassment about my poor label reading and get back to being lusty.

For those of you who are curious, I did end up moving back to the city and that bathroom has since been renovated. Lucky guy, and lucky me.

🖤

Spring Moons

B

How HR surprisingly helped my love life... and then less surprisingly didn't

This is the story of Ryan,
who came into my life

The same time as I was hiring
at work for my file.

To be clear,
he did not apply to work with me

That would be unethical
and a very different story.

No, he came through the usual app channel,

But I was feeling a bit experimental.

They say interviews are like first dates

But what if the entire dating experience
was like a recruitment process?

His Bumble resume had a few key words that
piqued my interest;

Our text screening revealed a few interests that I
wanted to further test.

Our first walking date showed what he cared for,
not much of which I cared for too deeply

But I was curious, I valued the ethics behind what
he cared for, and I had to remember,
Don't try to recruit people who are exactly like
you— seek complementary skills.

So yeah, unlike me, he was dependable, punctual,
spoke in direct uncaveated sentences

And he did have some core competencies
necessary for all team members, like a love for
mountains.

We even had follow-up interviews where key
skills and aptitudes were tested,

Including the openness to taking risks that are far greater than the reward.

A reference check was duly conducted with a mutual friend. No red flags.

A few further fun interviews in, he shared a paper he was writing.

The writing lacked the volume of winding sentences I favour

And also, the grammatical accuracy and logical argument I crave

But it had a greater purpose rooted in reality... and that I appreciated.

We didn't have an offer letter per se, but there was a general agreement

On general desires, challenges, and things that were good.

Really a recruitment process by the book!

But, alas, he did not last past the 3-month probationary period.

Circumstances changed for him and his responses to the challenges were different

Then in the initial set of interviews.

No matter the level of complexity in a simulated interview challenge

It's no comparison to real life.

Mother Earth

Yin Xzi Ho

In the spring of 2021, I was burnt out from graduating online and working from home, I decided to find a job in landscaping. I was determined to get myself outside and was entranced by the idea of working at a job that would involve me working with soil—being embedded in earth. I looked out my window at the tight fists of witch hazel flowers, waiting to bloom waiting to hop on a FaceTime interview with the person I hoped would be my boss, a powerful female owner of a landscaping company that loves to make gardens beautiful. By the time the magnolias had started to put out their first buds, I was hired! I bought myself my first pair of steel-toed boots and a new pair of wool socks

In my first couple of days I learnt a handful of useful skills—how to tie my boots up so that they didn't chafe the backs of my heels, how many layers of clothes to wear so that I could be warm in the morning and cool when afternoon heat set in, and how to watch my more experienced coworkers so that I could learn how they held their bodies in relation to the earth. It was exciting and invigorating to be outside after a year of feeling trapped inside behind a screen. With every sink of my shovel into the dirt, I felt myself rooting into this new lifestyle, and a little thrill inside me grew alongside my competence.

A week or so later though, I noticed the one thing that felt sticky. The way my boss had presented the company, I had come into landscaping with the impression that I would be working on a team of impassioned women, and so far, I was the only female body on a crew of four.

For the most part it was okay. Older than me by a decade or two, the men on the crew imbued the workplace with a certain degree of determined competition. It pushed me, the youngest at 22 (also the smallest member of the crew), to work harder and faster until I was shovelling soil amender, (a nutrient-rich alternative to mulch) at their pace and moving fast with a heavy wheelbarrow in my hands. I learnt how to maneuver a hydrostatic lawn mower around obstacles on my own (they're heavier than a regular mower because of its self-propelling the technology required to make it self-propelling). It came to a point where I felt like I thrived on this: the hustle and desire to get shit done.

We fell into a steady routine, waking up early in the morning in our respective homes to show up at my boss' place to load up the truck and trailer before 7 am every morning, hustling until noon to break for lunch, and then another four hours of work after lunch. I grew to like my crew and asked them large handfuls of questions every day so that I could gain from their landscaping experience. As we worked, I would pretend that we weren't that different—as the first set of people that I spent large quantities of time with outside of my household during the pandemic, it had become incredibly important to me that I fit in with my crew. Because of this, I mimicked their behaviors as well as I could, picking up on conversation cues that (when they departed from landscaping) circled around hockey, or the state of the Canadian government (something I knew very little about, having moved to Squamish from Malaysia). I set my personal goal as becoming the crew member to make the most dad jokes as possible, and I succeeded. As we worked alongside each other for 30-40 hours each week from March through April, I learnt how to hide the ways in which we were different —namely, my biology in comparison to theirs.

Landscaping around the townhomes in Squamish is tricky. Not because the plants that development companies choose to install are particularly hard to care for, though weeds can grow at mind-bendingly improbable rates. The difficulty lies in figuring out where to use the bathroom. As the only female member of the crew for the first handful of months of the landscaping year, I found it curious how my male coworkers never seemed to have a qualm about finding a corner to pee in. For the first month, I would walk into the woods around sites and squat, hoping that no dogs with curious noses would walk by. As time went by, I figured out my strategy for peeing at most sites. But there were still many places that I didn't dare pee, because I hadn't found the perfect spot yet.

One day in particular sticks with me, even now. It was a day in early April. We were having lunch at Talon, the strata (strata refers to individual property lots on common property, like townhouses). I liked peeing at Talon the least, because all of its seemingly hidden corners were right next to trails often walked on by people and their dogs, especially around lunch. I had finished my rice-vegetable-tofu combo of the day, and our half-hour lunch was drawing to a close. My bladder, which hadn't been relieved since 6:30 am, squeezed uncomfortably and I blurted out, "I gotta pee!"

Immediately embarrassed as everyone turned to face me, I put a grin on my face and chirped, "Be right back!" and tried to disappear behind the shrubbery. Now that I was in motion, it became of the utmost importance that I pee right now. None of the red osier dogwood shrubs around me had put on enough foliage to truly conceal me, but it didn't matter at that moment. I found a place to park myself so that only my head would be visible and frantically pulled at my belt in order to pee, making sure to catch my pruners (attached to my belt) before they hit the ground.

As I peed, I exhaled and closed my eyes, thankful that at least I had learnt how to use a Diva cup earlier in the year and could avoid having to change my pad in the outdoors. After my bathroom break, I made a mental note to try and time my water intake versus bladder output better, and I moved on with my day.

In May my boss hired more people for the team and my landscaping world, as I knew it, was upended. With five more people joining our crew of four, I was no longer the youngest, or the smallest, or the only female. Everything I had normalized about my body and what it should be able to do in relation to my manual labor job was called into question again.

With more women on the crew, I regularly had an extra pair of hands I could call on for help if I overfilled my bucket with heavy debris. And people would consult me for the best places to pee because they also had to squat. With more women on the team, I became useful outside of my landscaping skills. Suddenly my life experience was a helpful sounding board for day-to-day problems.

Surrounded by summertime roses and blooms that inspired Georgia O'Keeffe's yonic paintings, work talk started to include matters of the heart and uterus like never before. For a month, I couldn't go a day without birth control being brought up as a topic (sometimes in a silly manner, like, what if mosquitoes had birth control so we would have fewer mosquitoes? And sometimes in a way that held gravitas because it wasn't a hypothetical). We held council as we tended to garden beds across Squamish and the men on the crew started weeding farther and farther away from us. Often, on the weeks when our cycles were out of sync with each other, we stepped up for one another by pulling harder and working a little bit more for the woman who was experiencing cramps with little ability to obtain relief.

Bringing more women into the world of landscaping soothed my desire for a true connection to the land and the people around me in an unforeseen way. Suddenly, the natural functions, fluids, and appetites of my body were seen and validated. We laughed and healed each others' heartbreaks by spending hours spinning the stories of a love lost into something that we could talk about in a way that acknowledged ache but also allowed us to move on.

The fragrance of honeysuckle flowers and freshly turned earth helped turn our collaborative stories into a sort of medicine. A crew member's fear of spiders (and the subsequent discovery, while weeding, that spiders love making webs amongst the thorny branches of a rose bush) was eased by the giggling that happened as we teased each other. And those who weren't spider-shy offered to weed under those plants. Never would I have agreed to continue landscaping for another season if it weren't for the women who joined me in shaping the earth—who reminded me what it means to be a woman in relation to Mother Earth.

In the spring of 2022, I was re-hired by my landscaping team in the role of crew supervisor, after having worked my way through the entirety of the 2021 season as the only consistent crew member. In my introductory spiel to my new crew of mostly females, I recall the story of the time I gave myself a landscaping UTI from holding my pee too long when I was ensconced in my many layers of rain gear (one of which included a pair of overalls). I tell it as a warning story, and it usually resonates among the people I work with. It's a scenario which I can now whole-heartedly embrace and tell with pride, rather than keeping it to myself. I tell my crew to listen to me (so they don't accidentally cut themselves on any of the sharp tools), but also to listen to their bodies. If you need to pee—go pee!

Tomb Raider!

Pierre-Olivier Gaudreault

L'histoire que je m'apprête à vous raconter s'est déroulée en janvier 2018. C'est encore si frais. Vous savez, le genre de souvenirs qui vous replongent dans l'émotion comme si c'était hier? En plus d'avoir terminé mon emploi étudiant, je venais d'achever mon baccalauréat en géographie à l'Université McGill. Je criais « liberté »! J'étais envahi par un tel sentiment de complétude et de délivrance, au point où quasiment rien ne pouvait m'atteindre. J'avais enfin franchi la ligne d'arrivée d'un long marathon. Je me sentais fort, à un seul petit détail près : j'étais endetté. Qu'importe, j'avais du temps pour moi et je comptais en profiter avant de commencer à tout rembourser. De toute façon, une fois sur le marché du travail avec un diplôme universitaire, tout devrait s'arranger, non?... Jeune et naïf étais-je encore, mais ça, c'est une autre histoire!

Mon histoire a commencé quand j'ai décidé de m'offrir un voyage en cadeau après mes études. J'allais retrouver ma cousine, Mélina, qui pratiquait l'escalade près d'Antalya, en Turquie. À ce moment-là dans ma vie, ce projet frôlait presque la science-fiction. C'était littéralement une aventure à la Tomb Raider qui m'attendait. La fibre de globe-trotteuse et la passion pour l'aventure de Mélina m'avaient toujours fait rêver. J'étais au 7e ciel...

Première mésaventure : le vol. Je sais, c'est très commun pourriez-vous me dire! Mais ça vaut la peine de suivre l'histoire jusqu'au bout. À l'aéroport de Munich, la petite compagnie aérienne, SunExpress (le nom n'inspirait déjà pas vraiment le prestige), pour mon vol Munich-Antalya était incapable de trouver mon nom dans leur liste de passagers. À ma grande surprise, le reçu d'achat n'était pas suffisant comme j'avais réservé le vol auprès d'une agence de voyage en ligne du style Expedia. Aucun moyen de rejoindre Mélina qui devait me récupérer à l'aéroport dans quelques heures...Et, évidemment, aucun moyen de rejoindre l'agence à Montréal à 5h du matin non plus. Misère! Le ciel m'a finalement tendu une fleur. Ou un avion pour être plus exact! Cette année-là, les prix des vols en Turquie avaient baissé drastiquement à cause des instabilités politiques sous la gouverne d'Erdogan et de la guerre en Syrie qui empiétait sur l'Est du territoire de la Turquie. Ironiquement, c'était à la fois le bon et le mauvais moment de voyager en Turquie, selon les perspectives. Finalement, je m'en suis sorti en rachetant un nouveau billet d'avion pour seulement 100 Euros. La leçon : aucune, à part une histoire à raconter! C'est la vie!

Enfin, je suis arrivé à Antalya! À la fois fatigué et survolté, j'ai donc retrouvé ma cousine, ma Lara Croft. Étrangement, dès que je l'ai aperçue, j'ai eu l'impression que c'est moi qui serais supposé la rescaper...Ah! J'ai soudainement compris que j'allais tempérer l'ouragan qui se formait entre elle et son copain de l'époque. Ils ne sont plus ensemble aujourd'hui et pour cause, les ondes électromagnétiques supposément cancéreuses du routeur que son copain ne voulait pas installer. Le vase a fini par déborder...Certaines histoires romantiques ne durent qu'un chapitre, et d'autres, une vie. Comme quoi avoir le choix, c'est tout de même un privilège!? Le Wifi, c'est pratique après tout...non?

Tout roulait comme sur des roulettes. Outre l'escalade, c'est la Cappadoce et ses structures rocheuses en forme de phallus qui ont marqué mon imaginaire. "Pas surprenant", j'entends déjà me dire certains avec ironie! Mélina me redépose donc à l'aéroport d'Antalya. Prochaine destination, Istanbul le temps d'une fin de semaine avant de faire une escale de quelques jours à Paris chez d'anciens colocs avec qui j'avais habité à Montréal. La vie est belle, quoi! En attendant l'embarquement avec impatience, c'est le moment idéal de donner des nouvelles à ma mère...sauf qu'elle me prend complètement par surprise en m'annonçant son cancer du poumon. Le hamster se met à tourner à 100 km/h. Quel est le stade de son cancer? Va-t-elle s'en sortir? Dans le pire des scénarios, combien de temps lui reste-il à vivre? En sanglot et arrivant à peine à me parler, elle met fin à l'appel sans même que je puisse lui poser quelconque question. Tant pis! J'allais devoir combler le vide moi-même. Ma tentative de calmer mon anxiété s'est avérée plutôt contreproductive : chercher "cancer du poumon" sur Google! Dites-moi que vous auriez fait la même chose!? Assis dans l'avion, je m'efforçais de retenir mes larmes face à tous les scénarios possibles de mon imagination fertile. Et c'est là que la honte d'être aussi émotif devant des étrangers s'est emparé de moi. On m'a toujours appris qu'il faut éviter de pleurer en public. Je préférais résolument l'idée du jeune homme confiant, libre et heureux du début de l'histoire. Ma réalité avait changé : je me retrouvais comme un garçon vulnérable, seul et impuissant. Que faire? Je m'étais résolu à l'idée que le mieux à faire était de profiter du reste du voyage en m'occupant l'esprit.

À mon arrivée à Istanbul vers minuit, le conducteur de taxi m'a chargé le triple du prix habituel. « Ah! » Avec un goût d'amertume dans le fond de la gorge, je me suis rappelé ce que disait mon guide touristique : il faut négocier et faire attention aux arnaques. Je préférais passer l'éponge. Je n'avais pas l'énergie de confronter le conducteur. Ma tactique s'était révélée efficace, la beauté de la ville m'aidant à oublier l'accueil malhonnête que j'avais reçu et presque tout le reste, pour l'instant. J'étais ébahi par le mélange architectural et culturel diversifié d'Istanbul, une métropole riche d'une histoire sous les empires romain, byzantin et ottoman qui l'ont occupé autrefois. Elle est aussi réputée comme lieu symbolique par sa situation géographique à cheval entre l'Asie et l'Europe, les deux continents étant reliés par un pont qui traverse le détroit du Bosphore. Oups! Je n'avais aucun plan pour la soirée et le sentiment de solitude recommençait tranquillement à refaire surface.

Sauvé par la cloche! Alors que je marchais à travers la foule sur la place Taksim, la principale place publique de la cité, un homme du coin (que je surnommerai tout simplement l'homme (il-lui)) s'est approché pour me demander si j'avais un briquet. Après lui avoir répondu par la négative, il a enchaîné à me demandant je venais d'où, remarquant mon accent étranger. Une question en amenait une autre, et nous voilà en train de déambuler sur la place centrale. Pour l'extraverti que je suis, c'était agréable, la compagnie. Socialiser estompait mon sentiment de solitude et me changeait les idées. Il m'a ensuite invité à prendre un verre. Deux options : 1) lui donner le bénéfice du doute ou 2) écouter les sages recommandations de mon guide touristique. Évidemment, j'ai opté pour la première, mais mon instinct me disait d'être prudent même si tout le monde mérite une chance, à mon avis.

Assis au bar, je ne savais toujours pas si je pouvais lui faire confiance, encore moins s'il était intéressé par moi d'un point de vue amical ou romantique. À vrai dire, je n'arrivais pas à déterminer ce qu'il voulait du tout. D'un autre côté, la bonne compagnie tombait à point. J'ai donc laissé la naïveté triompher. Je n'avais rien à perdre. J'aimais qu'il s'intéresse à moi et qu'il semble sûr de lui. Prochaine étape, il m'a invité à aller en boîte de nuit. J'avais une boule dans la gorge, mais l'idée de retourner seul à mon auberge me paraissait encore pire. J'ai choisi le déni au lieu de la douleur. À la fois incertain et excité, j'ai embarqué avec lui dans le taxi. C'est l'aventure qui recommençait! Moi aussi, j'avais le droit d'avoir mon personnage dans Tomb Raider, me suis-je dit à moi-même!

Une fois à la boîte de nuit, l'homme en question m'a conduit à une banquette. Il a commandé à boire et à manger. Tout semblait présager un bon moment, jusqu'à ce que, évidemment, deux jeunes femmes vêtues de jupes courtes se joignent à nous et me coincent au fond de ladite banquette. Alors qu'il se vantait du fait que nous aurions la meilleure baise (traduction libre du mot "fuck") de notre vie cette soirée-là, la pression au niveau de mon abdomen s'intensifiait. Tout à coup, tout m'apparaissait clair comme de l'eau de roche. Ce que j'espérais être une rencontre romantique était devenu un cauchemar. La honte! Comme si la situation n'était déjà pas assez embarrassante, le serveur s'est approché pour gentiment m'informer que je devrais non seulement payer le plateau de nourriture et tout l'alcool que l'homme avait commandé, mais aussi la tonne de cocktails (more "mock", less "cock" svp!) que les deux femmes s'apprêtaient à commander. Bref, la fête allait être sur mon dos! Et là, un autre éclair de géni m'est venu : j'étais la victime de l'arnaque "Let's have a drink", exactement telle que décrite dans mon guide touristique. Du fait du contexte émotionnel dans lequel je me trouvais, j'avais ignoré les signes. Encore pire, j'avais ignoré mon instinct.

C'est bien beau se lamenter, mais il fallait bien que je me sorte de ce pétrin. Les jeunes femmes peu vêtues n'avaient clairement pas l'air intéressées par moi, et moi non plus en l'occurrence. Il m'est venu l'idée de faire semblant de chercher à l'intérieur de mon sac à dos de manière nerveuse et empressée, prétendant que j'avais oublié de prendre un médicament. C'était le seul stratagème que j'avais trouvé pour demander à mes prétendus nouveaux amis de se lever de la banquette afin que je puisse aller aux toilettes pour mieux voir dans mon sac sous la lumière. Devant le miroir, je réfléchissais en tournant en rond. 1, 2, 3, go! Et c'était parti, profitant du fait que la voie était libre, je me suis mis à courir à toute allure vers la sortie en haut des escaliers. Puis, j'ai sauté dans le premier taxi. Enfin sorti de ce calvaire, ma respiration s'est calmé...

C'est seulement avec un peu de recul que j'ai pris conscience de l'ampleur de ce qui c'était réellement passé. Force est d'admettre que j'aurais pu être agressé physiquement et dépouillé de tout mon argent. Cette expérience me rappelle la loi de l'impermanence : tout peut changer à tout moment. Une mauvaise nouvelle, un accident, la perte d'un être cher ou d'un emploi. Devant la vulnérabilité universelle, le moment présent est ce qu'il y a de plus précieux.

Quand l'adversité se présente, ce souvenir me rappelle d'aller chercher du soutien, et surtout de choisir les bonnes personnes. La personne en qui on peut avoir le plus confiance, c'est en nous-même, sauf peut-être lorsqu'une situation déstabilisante nous éloigne de notre sagesse intérieure. Mon instinct, un filet de sécurité social, les sensations de mon corps (qui ne mentent jamais d'ailleurs): tout y était pour me prévenir, à qui veut ou peut bien l'écouter!

Tomb Raider!

Pierre-Olivier Gaudreault

The story I'm about to tell you happened in January 2018. But it's still so fresh in my mind; you know, the kind of memories that plunge you back into the emotions of it as if it had only happened yesterday. In addition to leaving my student job, I had just completed my bachelor's degree in Geography at McGill University. I felt like screaming "freedom!" I was overwhelmed by such a sense of completeness and relief, to the point where almost nothing could affect me. I had finally crossed the finish line of a long marathon. I felt strong, except for one small detail—I was in debt. But I had time on my hands, money in my pocket, and I intended to enjoy it before paying it off. In any case, once I put my university degree to work and got a job in my field, everything would work out, right? I guess I was still naive and young, back then, but that's another story!

This story begins when I decided to gift myself a trip after graduation. I was going to meet my cousin, Melina, who was climbing near Antalya, Turkey. At that time in my life, this project was on the verge of science fiction. A Tomb Raider adventure was waiting for me. Melina's globetrotter spirit and passion for adventure had always made me dream. I was in seventh heaven. Little did I know what was to come.

The first mishap: the flight. I know, that's a fairly common one, you might say. But bear with me until the end. At the Munich airport, the small airline, SunExpress (the name already did not inspire confidence), for my Munich-Antalya flight was unable to find my name in their passenger list. To my surprise, the purchase receipt was not sufficient as I had booked the flight through an Expedia-style online travel agency. There was no way to reach Melina who was supposed to pick me up at the airport in just a few hours. And, of course, no way to reach the agency in Montreal at 5 a.m. either. Damn!

Lucky for me, I received a gift from the universe. That year, flight prices in Turkey had dropped drastically because of the political instabilities under President Recep Tayyip Erdoğan's rule and the war in Syria that was encroaching on the eastern part of Turkey's territory. Ironically, it was both a good and bad time to travel to Turkey, depending on whom you asked. In the end, I got away with buying a new plane ticket for only 100 Euros. The lesson: none, except for a good story to tell! *C'est la vie!*

Finally, I arrived in Antalya! Both tired and excited at the same time, I found my cousin, my Lara Croft. Strangely, as soon as I saw her, I had the impression that I was going to be the one doing the rescuing...Ah! I was suddenly aware that I was going to have weather the hurricane that was forming between her and her boyfriend at the time. They are not together due to her insistence on an installation of an internet router that supposedly emitted cancerous electromagnetic waves. This had been the final straw for both of them. Some romantic stories last only a chapter, and others, a lifetime. What a privilege to have a choice! Wi-Fi is useful after all...no?

Everything was going like clockwork. Besides the climbing, it was the Cappadocia trip extravaganza and its phallus-shaped rock structures that captured my imagination.

“What a surprise!” I heard people who know me well say ironically.

Melina dropped me off at the Antalya airport. My next destination, Istanbul for the weekend before stopping for a few days in Paris to visit former roommates I had lived with in Montreal. Life couldn’t be better!

While waiting for the flight, I thought it would be the perfect time to call my mother and share my most recent adventures with her. Except, she had news of her own: she took me by complete surprise announcing to me that she had been diagnosed with lung cancer. My mind began spinning at 100 km an hour, like a hamster running on a wheel.

What stage of cancer was she in?
Will she survive?

In the worst-case scenario, how long does she have to live?

Sobbing and barely able to speak to me, she ended the call without me even getting a chance to ask her any questions. I would have to fill the void myself. My attempt at calming my anxiety proved to be rather counterproductive: I Googled, lung cancer! You can't tell me you wouldn't have done the same thing! As I sat on the plane, I tried to hold back tears at all the possible scenarios that my active imagination was generating. And it was at this very moment that the shame of being so emotional in front of strangers took hold of me. I had always been taught not to cry in public. I definitely preferred the idea of the confident, free and happy young man at the beginning of the story. But my reality had changed: I found myself a vulnerable, lonely, helpless boy. What could I do? I resolved that the best thing to do was to enjoy the rest of the trip by keeping my mind busy.

After arriving in Istanbul around midnight, the cab driver charged me triple the usual price. It left a bitter taste in the back of my throat; I remembered what my guidebook had warned:

you must negotiate and be careful with scams. I would have to remember this for the next time. Right then, I didn't have the energy to confront the driver. So far, my tactic was proving effective, the beauty of the city helped me forget the dishonest welcome I had received, my mother's sad news and almost everything else, for the time being. I was amazed by the architectural and cultural diversity of Istanbul, a metropolis rich in history under the occupation of the Roman, Byzantine and Ottoman Empires. It is also known as a symbolic place because of its geographical location straddling Asia and Europe; the two continents being connected by a bridge across the Bosphorus Strait.

As I was walking through the crowd in Taksim Square, the main public square of the city, I realized I had no plans for the evening, and suddenly my feeling of loneliness began to resurface. However, maybe my luck was about to change. A local man approached me and asked me if I had a lighter. After answering him in the negative, he went on to ask me where I was from, noticing my foreign accent. One question led to another, and there we were, strolling around the central square. For the extrovert that I am, the company felt quite pleasant. Socializing made me feel less lonely and helped me take my mind off things. The man then invited me for a drink. In my mind I had two options: give him the benefit of the doubt or I could listen to the wise recommendations of my guidebook and refuse invitations made by random strangers. Obviously, I opted for the former, but also followed my instinct to remain cautious even though in my opinion, everyone deserves a chance.

Sitting at the bar, I still didn't know if I could trust him, let alone if he was interested in me in a friendly or romantic way. Truth be told, I couldn't figure out what he wanted at all. On the other hand, good company was just what I needed. I decided I had nothing to lose. So, I let naivety win. I liked his confidence and his attention. Next, he invited me to go to a nightclub. I had a lump in my throat, but the thought of going back to my hostel alone felt even worse. I chose denial over pain. Uncertain and excited at the same time, I got into the cab with him. It was the thrill of adventure all over again! I too had the right to play my own character in Tomb Raider, I thought to myself.

Once at the nightclub, the man led me to a seat. He ordered food and drinks. It all seemed to bode well for a good time, until, of course, two young women dressed in short skirts and cropped tops joined us and cornered me in the back of the booth. The man leaned over to me and bragged that we were going to have the "best fuck of our lives" that night. I felt the pressure in my abdomen intensify. Suddenly, everything was crystal clear. What I had hoped would become a romantic encounter had become a nightmare. I felt so ashamed! As if the situation wasn't embarrassing enough, the waiter kindly informed me, while clearly putting pressure on me, that I would not only have to pay for the tray of food and all the alcohol that the man had already ordered, but also for all of the cocktails that the two women had ordered. In short, the party was going to be on my back!

At that moment, I realized: I was the victim of the "Let's have a drink" scam, exactly as described in my guidebook. Because of the emotional context I was in, I had ignored all the red flags. Even worse, I had ignored my instincts. It was all very well to feel sorry for myself, but I had to get out of this mess. The scantily clad young women clearly didn't seem to be interested in me, nor I in them for that matter. But it was also at that moment that a plan came to mind. A flash of genius that Lara Croft, my favourite action-adventure character would herself be proud of.

I began to rummage around inside my backpack, in a nervous and hurried manner, pretending that I had forgotten to take medication. It was the only ploy I could come up with to get my so-called new friends to let me leave the table. I told them I needed to go to the bathroom where there was more light and I could search my bag. I stood in front of the mirror; my mind was going in circles. Could I actually pull this off? I counted 1, 2, 3, go! And bolted out of the bathroom. I ran at full speed towards the exit at the top of the stairs and ran outside, jumping in the first cab I saw. As the cab made its way back to the hostel, my breathing became calmer and my heart had finally stopped pounding.

It is only with a little hindsight that I realized the extent of what had really happened. It scares me to think of what could have happened. I could have been robbed or even worse physically assaulted. When I think about it, the experience reminds me of the law of impermanence: everything can change at any time. Bad news, an accident, the loss of a loved one or a job. In the face of universal vulnerability, the present moment is the most precious thing we have. When adversity strikes, this memory not only reminds me to reach out for support, but more importantly, to choose the right people. The person we can trust the most is ourselves, except perhaps when a destabilizing situation takes us away from our inner wisdom. My instinct, a social safety net, my body's sensations (which never lie by the way), were all there to warn me, all I had to do was be willing to listen!

B

A Matter of Definitions

My standards for Bumble dating in the prairies are quite low. Just seeing a guy with a shirt on, without a fish, and without gym-toned biceps is enough to catch my attention. Dean didn't just meet those criteria, but he also said he was a nerd and that he liked to read. It only took a few text messages before we decided to meet. The timing was great as Beakerhead was happening in town. Beakerhead is this amazing merging of art, science, and play. There were several fun and interactive installations, all along the beautiful Bow River. It was the perfect setting to get to know a fellow nerd and have fun at the same time, or so I thought.

We found each other easily and once the awkward hi's were done we started walking around Beakerhead. I found out he was really into video games and read mostly comic books—that's great by me, even though I don't have the skill or aptitude for either of those. Also, he wasn't really into science. He didn't want to stop at any of the installations.

I somehow convinced him to try out one experiment booth, and he did not enjoy it at all. And he made sure that both I and the volunteers at the booth knew that. Maybe he had had a rough day, prior to meeting. Maybe someone accidentally stepped on his favourite video game CD or cassette. Thankfully we parted ways after what was an excruciating two hours for both of us.

Either way it was the first time in my life that I did not feel joy at a science and art show. The whole time, as I tried to engage him at the different science installations and booths, I tried to think about how this could go so sideways. To me a nerd is just someone who is passionate about something and who loves to learn. I take it to mean that they must obviously get excited by art and/or science. There was so much of Dean's personality I had built in my own head without realizing it. The Dean that resided in my head was this curious guy who would be thrilled to look at and learn about cool things that shine and move in unexpected ways. He read books about science, the universe, and human nature. Also, he was inexplicably curious to know more about me, good at asking perceptive questions, and adventurous.

While I'm embarrassed to admit that I had attributed all these conclusions from his profile without much evidence, I do wish Bumble would develop some standardized definitions for adjectives used in profiles. Just so we're all on the same page regarding the words we use to describe ourselves, like "nerd". Or maybe, I just need to ask better questions via text...

A Sock in a Dark Place

Kayley Fesko

I'd only been a mother for 10 hours when I realised something was wrong. The labour had been extremely long and stressful. Our doula had told my husband to go home so he could get some rest and be ready to help take care of me and our new baby when we came home.

I had just finished nursing and had settled my baby and stood up to make my way to the hospital washroom, trying to be as quiet as possible so as not to disturb the other family sharing the room, who had just welcomed their second baby into the world. As I stood up and made my move towards the washroom I started peeing uncontrollably. No bladder control whatsoever.

I felt my face turn red and I panicked as I watched the puddle of urine expand beneath me. "I'm sorry. I'm so sorry. I can't stop it. It won't stop." I said towards the other bed enclosed in curtains.

There was no response from the couple next to me. But as the pee began to spread, her partner silently moved their duffle bag out of the puddle's way. Still no response or reassurance from either of them. I was mortified.

I really didn't want to ring the bell to tell the nurse I'd peed all over the floor. Not just a small pee but like I-drank-10-litres-of-water-in-a hour-and-it's-all-coming-out-at-once amount of pee. I took a blanket off the hospital bed and soaked up the pee as best I could. Then I walked with my baby, my head hung low, to go find a nurse to tell her the unfortunate news.

What felt like hours passed, waiting for the janitorial staff to come clean up the blankets and wash the floor. Fatigued, alone, and in a sterile hospital, with no one I love around me except this new being, anxiety started settling in like fog on a moor.

Even on that first day of motherhood, I felt alone. I tried desperately to connect with the mom on the other side of the curtain, but it remained closed for the rest of my stay. I wanted so badly to talk about peeing on the floor with someone who could empathise. I sat there alone and thought, is this what motherhood is really about? Will it ever improve? What happened down there? The lovely thing about anxiety is that these questions quickly spiral into a dramatic story leaving me with the idea that I would forever need a catheter to keep myself from peeing on the next person's duffle bag and that I would be without someone to talk with about it for the rest of my life.

Once I got home, in the arms of my loving partner, I was able to settle my mind. I told myself that I likely won't be peeing on anyone's bag. It's going to get better. It can't get worse right?

I began to settle into my new role of being a mom and as other priorities took over, I had long forgotten about my incident in the hospital. My focus was on getting to know this new, little being that was so squishy and oh so cute. Soon, my adventures expanded from checking to see what's in the fridge, to exploring the street and beyond. By this time, I was able to hold my pee a bit better although I would still pee my pants occasionally—No big deal, I could handle a little pee. After all, I had just overcome months of mastitis (inflammation of breast tissue). But, I'll save that story for another day.

One day, while I was walking with my son and my dog up a hill on my way back home, I felt something between my legs. It felt heavy, like a saturated tampon slowly slipping out or a balled up sock that I forgot to sort out when folding laundry. Concerned, I started walking faster to get home so I could check what was actually going on. When I got home, I immediately raced into the washroom and a sudden urge to pee. It was the most satisfying pee I've ever had. It felt so relieving. But, as I went to wipe, that's when I felt it—my bladder protruding out of my body. Like a little puzzle piece. I spent a few moments trying to push it back into its proper place. Once satisfied, I stood up only for it to fall right back out when I tried to pick up my son. Now, I'm not an expert but I *knew* that this wasn't supposed to be happening but given my experience with my pre and postnatal care, I just kept it quiet in fear that I would be dismissed. Again.

The rest of the year I quietly asked questions to mothers I met, hoping someone would open up about their experiences down there. Are you having sex? Are you healed? Are you having trouble with controlling your bladder? Has your bladder fallen out? I was frustrated to find women didn't want to talk about the weird and sometimes shocking things that happen to our bodies after childbirth, or even the experience of trying to have sex after childbirth. I had expected women to be more willing to share, instead it felt like we were all trying to perpetuate this clean, perfect experience:

We've had sex already. Everything is all healed up. I don't feel comfortable talking about this.

Why do we always want to talk about the perfect things in our lives and not the things that we need to hear? I was looking for someone who was willing to share. To admit that their bladder, or their vagina, or their rectum had fallen out, or at the very least someone to say, "Yes! I know exactly what you're talking about."

Finally, I found someone. She had been part of my prenatal yoga classes and gave birth a few months after me. When she finally felt strong enough to get together, she was able to dish about all the trauma, organs, experts, and lessons she had learned along the way. It only took one person to make me feel like I was being heard and listened to. A person who could put me on the right track to start exploring different options for support. A person who was so willing to dive right into the dark side of birth and the postpartum experience. I still feel forever grateful for this person.

After our conversation, I eagerly called a pelvic floor physiotherapist clinic and spoke with the receptionist. I was excited at the thought of finally getting my body back to some kind of normal. I was thinking it would take maybe a week, maybe two weeks. Then the receptionist very calmly and matter-of-factly informed me that the first available appointment would be in 10 months. 10 MONTHS! That's a long time to wait with your bladder hanging between your legs.

When I finally did get my first appointment with the pelvic floor physiotherapist, I was diagnosed with a stage three pelvic organ prolapse. That's a scale, based on four stages, to say how far your organs are hanging down from where they should be. Stage three is not a great place to start from. The pelvic floor physiotherapist was incredible—she gave me exercises that I could do anywhere I wanted to. When I went out for a bike ride, I would stop at a red light and breathe through a few exercises—close the "gondola doors", ride up the gondola, go back down the gondola, and open the doors slowly. And repeat. With motivation and newfound knowledge, I told everyone about doing their Kegel exercises. I would take Kegel breaks at work, on walks, and when hanging out with friends. Even my partner got into it and built me a stool for each washroom in our house so I could have the proper sitting technique when going about my business.

Queue second child. I'm ready to give birth, in a way that will protect my pelvic floor. My midwives know how important this is to me. The doula that supported me postpartum reminded me to do my exercises. I saw the physiotherapist early on. I was doing all the right things. My bladder was sitting in the right place before and after birthing a 9 lb 6 oz baby. Success!

Given my experience postpartum with my first child, I was scared to return to doing activities that I did freely before children. I avoided running, jumping, lifting, carrying items, and intense physical exercise in order to avoid straining the muscles holding up my pelvic organs. Most days I didn't miss the intense exercise, I was too tired anyway.

When my youngest was two and my eldest was five, we bought them a trampoline. They loved it. They spent hours jumping and giggling. I found the giggle-inducing trampoline too hard to resist and one day, I decided to join in the fun. Two jumps in, I felt something. A familiar feeling. One that I hadn't felt in a long time. The sock was back.

A week later, I was back at the physiotherapist. This time was different, I had the same stage of prolapse, but the exercises were no longer supporting me the way I needed them to. She referred me to the Women's Health Clinic for more support.

I arrived at the clinic for my appointment and was surprised to find that it was in the basement of an older building on the hospital campus. There were no windows which made it feel dark and dingy, like no one really cared about this part of the healthcare system. I thought I was going to be met by a grumpy nurse with outdated information. Instead, I met nurses who were extremely motivated to support me. They listened to me, heard all my concerns, and allowed me to show up as my true self.

At my first appointment, I was fitted with a pessary. For those of you who aren't aware, a vaginal pessary is a removable silicone device that is placed into the vagina to hold everything in its proper spot. Once in, the nurse asked me to relax all my muscles and jump up and down, run down the hallway, do all the things that I hadn't been able to do in years. At that moment, I started crying—but this time tears of joy. After six years of struggling to control my bladder, of not being able to jump without peeing my pants or having my pelvic organs fall out of my body, I was jumping and running and not a drop of pee, or that feeling of having a sock between my legs. I was so happy that I hugged the nurse. I had dreamt of a day when I could run after my children without having to immediately rush home to push my bladder back up into my body. And finally, it felt like that day was here. All thanks to this tiny little piece of silicon in my vagina. While it's not a fix-all-solution, it's a very helpful tool that I can use to help support my pelvic floor.

Reflecting back on this story six years later, I can't help but wonder why no one once talked about pelvic floor health during my pregnancy? During delivery? Or postpartum after I shamefully told the nurse that I had peed all over the floor? Not once. In many countries pelvic floor physiotherapy can be a part of your pre and postnatal care (if you choose). So, to all the women reading this story—old, young, with or without kids—this is a reminder to do your Kegels. If you're pregnant, do some research and ask as many questions as you can think of about your pelvic floor. And if you're postpartum and things don't feel right, don't be shy, don't stay quiet—have the courage to ask for the support that feels right for you. And if you're having trouble finding the support, don't give up—if it doesn't feel right, it isn't.

Summer Moons

Heather Hendrie

Should I write about how I hooked up with a guy named Manuel Antonio in Manuel Antonio?

In the town of Manuel Antonio, I once hooked up with a guy named Manuel Antonio.

I mean, what are the chances?

(I won't bother with the deep dive I could do here into what happens when you overlay patriarchy onto the still-too-present culture of machismo that pervades much of Latin America. Let's just say that in my sample size of <too many> I believe I have debunked the myth of the glory of the "Latin lover".

It would seem that being good at salsa dancing does not translate to attunement—or perhaps more accurately, giving a shit about the other person—in bed or beyond, and let's not even get started on abnormal pap smears.)

When Nature Calls

Paris

It was the kind of first date that I would force myself to go on when I had already met someone else that I liked. Definitely driven by a pattern of self-sabotage, but also that terrible, hard-to-resist-urge, fuelled by the accessibility and very nature of dating apps, to just make sure there wasn't someone out there who I might like a little more. I had been on a couple dates with Grady and was starting to really like him. We weren't exclusive yet, so there I was on Bumble agreeing to meet up with Paul, just to make doubly sure that I was really into Grady. So not a great decision to begin with.

Paul only had one photo of himself on his dating profile and didn't really say much in his bio either. Looking back, I can't exactly remember why I agreed to meet up with him with so little to go on. It might have had something to do with the hipster glasses he was wearing in his one photo—I'm a sucker for a thick frame.

For our date, we had agreed to meet at a coffee shop by my house and go for a walk along the river. It was well into October and the forecast did not look promising. Relieved, I thought this might make for a short and sweet date, provide an easy out. My reluctance to go on this date, which was high to begin with, was now growing by the minute.

As I walked to the coffee shop, big wet snowflakes started drifting slowly from the sky. Paul was waiting for me outside, dressed completely inappropriately for the weather. Sneakers and a thin jacket. This seemed to bode well for my escape plan. Missing were the hipster glasses from his profile picture. Which brought the number of things I found attractive about him down to about zero.

We ordered warm drinks and headed back outside, where the slowly falling snow had turned into a complete white-out in minutes. Ducking under the awning of a local drugstore we decided to huddle for a few minutes and see if we could wait it out. As soon as we were out of the snow, he turned to me with instant bedroom eyes, up-and-downed me and said,

"My, my, my, Paris, what a beautiful name for a beautiful girl. Tell me, how is someone like you still single?"

Now let me just pause here for a minute to express how much I hate that question. And also, how much I hate the instant discomfort of a virtual stranger you just met online coming onto you within minutes of first meeting. Major. Squirm.

So, at this point, I'm thinking, this guy is not ticking any of my boxes. He doesn't seem to be the most outdoorsy type, which is usually pretty important to me, he's a smoker, and he's uncomfortably flirtatious. And to be honest, I'm just not feeling this. I decide I'm going to try and wrap this date up in an hour or less.

No such luck.

Cut to an hour later—we've done a loop of the river, pausing only for him to smoke several cigarettes. During a lull in conversation I seamlessly segue into asking him where he parked. My luck has changed, he's parked less than a block from where we've found ourselves! I steer us in that direction, intending to walk him to his car. But as we approach his car he says, "maybe we could just walk for a half an hour longer?" Nothing in my being wants to say yes to this. I want to go home, run a bath, and stay in it forever.

I say yes.
Half an hour later we are sitting in a park by my house. He's asking me who else I've met online lately, how I'm ranking them, if I have a spreadsheet, and where he falls in all of it. The bedroom eyes are a constant now. I squint up at the suddenly bright sky, trying to will the usually welcome sunshine to just GO AWAY! Where are my friends, the snowflakes when I need them? Finally, I can't take it anymore, and I tell him I have somewhere to be in half an hour and that I'll walk him back to his car. We're half a block from my house but I don't want him to know where I live.

As we walk back towards the coffee shop where this whole saga began, he suddenly goes quiet and then says, "Uh I need a bathroom."

"No problem," I say, "I'm sure you can use the one in the coffee shop."

Now, at this point we have been outside in the fresh air for about two hours. We've walked by the river, we've sat in the park, we've passed at least a dozen small local businesses. There has been ample opportunity to duck into a local shop to use the restroom, or even behind a bush if need be. We've had coffee, it's chilly outside, and we're living through a global pandemic that has forced online dating into one long-ass outdoor walk. I would not have blinked an eye if he had excused himself to relieve himself, either indoors or outdoors, at any point on this date.

I think you might be starting to get where this is going.

As we cross a very public street, half a block from the coffee shop, I'm telling him about something, I can't remember what, when I suddenly hear him say, "Oh shit." I turn towards him and see a dark wet patch slowly spreading down the leg of his acid-wash jeans. He tries to turn away from me as I say, "Are you alright?"

And then in the blink of an eye, he just turns and runs—literally sprints away from me, down a side street, leaving me standing on the corner blinking, stunned, and questioning whether that ACTUALLY just happened. This bedroom-eyed stranger, with all his swag, has just peed his pants on our first date and then fled.

I take out my phone and send him a message: *Hey, not sure if you're coming back so I'm going to go, hope you're okay.*

Four hours later he responds: *All good. Sorry, nature called, had to run.*
All good, I respond, thinking that's the last I'll hear from him. Because really, how do you come back from that?
Three weeks later, my phone pings— a Bumble message from Paul: *Hey beautiful, how have you been?*

I don't reply for a few hours. I'm crafting a response in my mind that says something along the lines of, *It was nice to meet you, all the best, thanks but no thanks*, in the kindest possible way.

I open the app to respond.
He's unmatched with me.

The Summer of Yes

Paris

It's the summer after a big heart squeezing disappointment and I'm determined to put myself back out there. I harden myself against rejection. I will say yes to any date. I will swipe yes on any person who does not give me murder-y vibes. Discernment is out the door. Being a yes-person is in.

My first yes is a date with Cal, the Christian house painter. I've decided, in order to keep track of all the interesting types I say yes to, I will nickname them with one or two salient details about their lives to help me keep them all straight in my mind. As the nickname suggests, Cal is quite devoutly religious, and he is painting houses professionally for the summer. He's not the type that I might normally go for, but I'm a yes-person now so it doesn't even matter.

It's July and I have a hot date—literally. It's blisteringly hot outside, the sky a piercing blue and the heat creating a desert mirage-like shimmer over the sidewalks as the sun beats down. Cal and I matched on Bumble and quickly agreed to meet up, neither of us being much for long endless texting. He's invited me to join him for a game of disc golf in a popular park by the river. I've never played before—another easy yes. I'm supposed to meet him at the first hole, and by the time I get there, sweat is running down my back. I'm expecting him to look a certain way from his online profile—brown hair, a shadow of a beard, bright blue eyes, and I don't see anyone matching that description in the vicinity. I decide to give him a call to make sure I'm in the right place. He answers and I see a tall gangly man in the distance hurrying towards me waving one arm in the air while he holds the other to his ear. It's Cal. He's not how I had pictured him. He's very tall, quite shy and a little dorky. I feel like he might take some figuring out, but we've got a whole, hot, summer's afternoon stretched out before us to do just that.

There's a crowd of people gathered at the first hole, and we join it as Cal gives me the *Coles Notes* on the game. We get in line waiting to throw our first discs. The line is several groups deep, and as we inch forward slowly, I feel someone tap me lightly on the shoulder. I turn around, wondering who I know who might be a secret disc golf aficionado. To my surprise it's an elderly gentleman of no such acquaintance. He's wearing grey shorts in a faded sweat pant material, a white shirt tucked in at the drawstring waist, and white socks pulled up high under old white sneakers.

"Are you guys alone?" he asks.

I let out a surprised little laugh and say, "Well no, we're together," gesturing between me and the Christian house painter.

"Great," he says, "I'm Dave, I think I'll join you for a few rounds."

Cal and I blink at each other, but neither of us say a word or make a sound of protest, both too polite (any maybe stunned) to turn this man down. It's a beautiful day. It's our first date. We met literally five minutes ago for the first time ever. And now Dave is on our date too.

And so, it goes for the next hour. Dave confidently marching ahead, his soft white hair lifting gently with the blessed breeze as we make our way around the course.

Dave also quickly takes it upon himself to become my disc golf coach.

"Now see here, Paris, look at that guy there, in the red hat. See how he's angling the disc up like that when he throws? Try that on your next turn."

He shakes his head ruefully when my throws land woefully short of their target. "Oh Paris, you think by now you'd be getting the hang of it."

He sidles over to me at the 7th hole, "Paris, I've been watching your form the last two holes and you're still angling your wrist all wrong."

I spend more time being coached by Dave than in conversation with Cal. Polite, reserved Cal. Too kind to tell this man that he's crashing our first date. Too gentle to interrupt him with any of his own advice, allowing Dave, instead, to dominate the date.

We arrive at the 9th hole red-cheeked and slightly out of breath. We're halfway through the course and I can feel the heat stroke coming on strong. I'm about to suggest we find a shady spot for a little break, when Cal the Christian house painter turns to me and says, "So what do you do for work, Paris?"

Dave, within earshot, whips his head around, his sharp blue eyes darting from me to Cal, Cal to me. He clears his throat, and I can see, an hour and forty-five minutes into railroading this date, that it has suddenly dawned on him that he's landed himself in a capital 'S' situation—that he is third-wheeling on a game between two people who have only just met.

He looks up at the summer-blue sky and then back down at the parched grass, gives his head a little shake and says, "You know guys, I think I'm just going to throw nine today. You finish without me. I'm going to tap out here."

I thought I would feel relief when the moment that three became two finally came around, but now as I watch Dave walk away putting his discs back into his little plastic carrier bag with his water bottle and snacks, I feel a pang of grief pierce my chest and have a sudden urge to call him back and tell him it's okay, we want you here. We've been enjoying your company. Please stay. Because I had been enjoying his company. He added some delight, hilarity, and personality to an otherwise stilted first date between two people with little in common.

As we watch him walk away Cal says, "I think maybe he just came out today hoping for some company. Life can be lonely sometimes."

My heart squeezes a little as I nod my agreement and blink back an unexpected tear. Life can be lonely sometimes. And maybe Dave was just the thing that my sad, lonely heart needed today, with his unsolicited dad advice and disc golf dominance. His brave insertion into the meeting of two strangers, and his just-as-gracious exit upon realising his mistake.

I didn't see Cal the Christian house painter again after that date, but I saw people that I mistook for Dave everywhere that summer. People just looking for connection in a pandemic-weary world.

Being a yes-person starts to wear a bit thin by the end of the summer, and discernment is strapped firmly back into the driver's seat of my dating life, but I try to smile more at strangers, and keep an openness to my spirit when I'm out in the world. Just in case one day I encounter another Dave, hoping for someone to look up and catch his eye with some kindness; someone to help him feel not so lonesome, for just a little while.

april joseph

One + One = Three

when one and one make three
three craves to be one to seek
a starlit split comes into view
simultaneous death and (re)birth
an all-seeing eye
two songs sing the ache of love

Out of love
is not the same *anda errante*
Holding onto remains *con las almas*
de los muertos[1]

---

[1] *"Anda errante con las almas de los muertos" is from Gloria Anzaldúa's poem, "My Black Angelos" in Borderlands/ La Frontera: The New Mestiza.*

awfully hilarious

words are not enough
to release
stone surround us
fire starved
drowning out

Yours. My.
Luz

To choose: we're not the same
Excusing ourselves

to be
out of love

is not the same
anda errante
con las almas
de los muertos

Luz
is not
the same

allows us to dream
the thread
binds us to
sew

in two
Luz

awfully hilarious

is not the same   *is not*
                    the same

let tears bury los muertos
raise the heart to gather new voices
Luz

merge and break the illusion of one
and one merge in two

Autumn Moons

The Curse of the Tiny Toilet

Grace Davies

As a parent, the glorious toddler years can be filled with so many fun moments. The first steps they take on their own, or the first time they tell you, "I love you mama" can just absolutely melt your heart. Not only are the toddler years filled with joy, they're also filled with some not so fun stuff—like potty training. This second time around through the toddler years, I have to say that I considered myself to be an "experienced mother" or in other words an "expert mother". My little guy is my second child, and I thought I had been through this all before with my now pre-teen daughter. Ha! Little did I know!

I decided to begin the potty-training process with my little guy earlier, rather than later. This time I'll get a jump start, I thought, because I knew so much better now. Potty training was sure to be a breeze this time around—because I was a Super Mom now. I had it all under control, or so I thought.

Before my son was even able to stand, a family member purchased him a tiny toilet, as a gift, that looked exactly like the classic toilet model. This toilet was perfect. It had the shiny, pearly white toilet seat that goes up and down just like a regular one. It had its own small toilet paper dispenser, and it even had a chrome-looking silver flusher that, when pushed down, made a sound like a real toilet flushing. I was sure my toddler would ditch his diapers and trade them for his very own tiny toilet when the time came—without hesitation.

So, as planned when he turned one, I decided to put the tiny, shiny toilet right next to the big toilet in my bathroom. That way, when he followed me into the bathroom every time I used the big toilet (and you know, as a parent to a toddler you're never going to the bathroom alone), I knew he would want to copy me, as he so often does, by sitting on (and hopefully using) his own tiny toilet. This plan was foolproof, or so I thought.

As I expected, not long after seeing me use the big toilet over and over again and seeing his own identical small version of a toilet, he wanted to start sitting on it too. His first pee came when he was only 14 months old. In my mind, it was confirmed at that moment: I *was* Super Mom! My one-year-old was using the toilet; I was surely superior to all other parents. I even thought to myself, I should write a book or a blog post or something.

As months went by, and he'd had his second birthday, he was still using his tiny toilet like a champ. But I began to notice that when we were out running errands or doing things outside of the house he was still peeing and pooping in his pants. This was becoming an issue, not only because I was growing tired of scrubbing poo from his little underpants, or that I was constantly doing laundry, but also because I was slowly starting to feel like my Super Mom cape was starting to tear. He was great at using his tiny potty but when we weren't at home, he absolutely refused to use a full-size public toilet. Every time

I tried to sway him to try to use a regular size toilet he would tell me, "Not the big potty Mommy, I need my tiny toilet." I even tried to put a little toilet seat on the big toilet seat, but that didn't work. While my plan to get him potty-trained at a young age worked, it seemed like my once brilliant plan had backfired on me. All he wanted was a tiny toilet and they didn't have those in public restrooms (yet!)

After assessing the situation, the only thing that made sense to me was to carry the tiny toilet with us wherever we went. At least until I could somehow get him to use a regular toilet. So, that's exactly what I did. Once again, my plan was working effortlessly. He was going potty in public when we were out and about, and not having any accidents in his pants. Sure, I had to pull a tiny toilet out on the side of the road, or in the school pick-up line for my daughter, or in the parking lot—in plenty of parking lots, but I didn't care. It was worth it—it was working!

One fine morning my son and I were spending some time together after dropping my eldest child off at school. It was a Wednesday, and Wednesdays are our designated library day. The library wasn't open until 10:00 a.m., so we had some time to kill. We stopped to get a bite to eat at a new bagel shop in town, and then headed toward the library. As I was pulling into the library parking lot, I suddenly felt a massive churn in my stomach and a tight clench in my rear.

At that moment I knew something bad was coming. I had to squeeze the cheese, unloose the caboose, or perhaps a less frowned-upon way to say, I had to answer nature's call. Whatever you want to call it, this crap was coming, and fast. This was unlike most other times I've had to go, where there would be warning signs. This time there weren't any warning signs or even some sort of build up to the grand finale. It was like I skipped all the light contractions and went into full blown labour (with a little log baby).

Normally there would be an easy solution, just grab my son and run into the library like my life depended on it and find myself a toilet. Except there was one major problem; the library was still closed. It was only 9:50—it wasn't going to be open for another 10 minutes, leaving me in a really shitty situation, one might say.

Trying not to panic, I parked the car and nervously looked at the clock. It was 9:52. I took a deep breath and I started to pep talk myself out loud saying things like, "Alright girl you got this! Eight minutes is nothing!" But then I felt my stomach churn and I once again felt a tight pressure coming from my butt cheeks. Suddenly eight minutes feels like a thousand years from now.

As we sat in the car waiting, I danced around in my seat. I looked at the clock, and it read 9:53. Only one minute has passed! Seriously? I'm getting more desperate by the second. And desperate times, call for desperate measures. I look around the parking lot for a spot where I can drop this load. There was a park by the library, but no public toilets, or any place that I could go with a half-way decent amount of privacy. I grow more and more desperate by the second. I mean, as a mother of two children, I'm all-too familiar with bodily fluids and public releases, but the indignity of shitting oneself as an adult is too much. I looked around desperately, catching sight of the whites of my own eyes in my rear-view mirror, and that's

when I saw it, the tiny toilet! Easily reachable. Easily accessible. A toilet at my fingertips.
Without questioning consequence, I hopped out of the front seat faster than I've ever done and hopped into the back seat. As I grabbed the tiny toilet and placed it on the back seat, I said to my son "Sorry honey Mommy has to use your tiny toilet—I have to go potty so bad!"
I see his eyes grow as big as golf balls and they began to water.

"No Mommy! Don't do it!" His little eyes and his hurt voice struck a chord that slapped me from my state of desperation, back to reality.

"Okay, you're right," I said to him.

What am I doing? I think to myself. Don't be crazy, the library will be open in five minutes. I can hold it. My pants were already halfway down, so I try to hold on to any pride I have left and yank them back up. I open the back seat car door for privacy and attempt to hectically zip up my pants. Maybe standing will make it more bearable.
So, here I am standing and attempting to zip up my zipper whilst holding my butt cheeks as tight

as possible. I get my zipper all the way up and grab my son out of the car when I feel some serious pressure again. This time there was no turning back, it was coming, and I couldn't stop it no matter how much I tried. I quickly grabbed my son and threw him in his car seat as I blurted out, "Nope, this can't wait, it's happening NOW—sorry buddy!" I hop back in, pull my pants down faster than I ever have and let loose into the tiny potty.

My son, sitting right beside me in his car seat, begins crying, "MOMMY NOOOOOO! NOT MY TINY POTTY! NOOOOOO, MOMMY..." repeatedly.

It was too late though, there was nothing I could do except say as I gasped for breath, "Sorry buddy, Mommy tried." The crap flowed from me like hot lava as I shamelessly shat on that tiny toilet. For a second, I thought about how I may overflow this tiny little pot and on to the car, but at this point I didn't care. My son was sobbing, and I was just going to have to deal with whatever "shit" I stirred up after I was done.

Finally, after what seemed like a minute or two it stopped. I looked, and luckily, I didn't overflow that tiny toilet. I mean wow, it could have been worse, right? Not much worse, but still. While sitting on the top of a tiny toilet on the top of my back seat I leaned over to grab my son's diaper bag and his wipes. I thought to myself, thank god these were in here. Who knew I'd be wiping my own butt with them? I wiped myself and fell to the floor of my car—my pants weren't even pulled up all the way as I uncomfortably lay on the ground of my car laughing and crying at the same time while my son continued to sniffle saying, "Mommy, how could you?"

Seriously though, how could I not?

I had to dispose of the evidence and discreetly took the mess I made in the tiny toilet and dumped it behind a bush outside of the library. I managed to pull myself together and calm my son down. I sat there in the car, for a moment, pondering the state of my life. My Super Mom cape was now fully in tatters, and somewhat shit stained. After that, my little guy and I tried to salvage the day while I hoped nobody in the library had caught a glimpse of the actual shit-show outside.

Parachute Boy

alternate titles: Unhinged; or That Red Bag is Kind of a Red Flag

Heather Hendrie

I hadn't been on a date in a long time when I met Parachute Boy, and I'm pretty sure it was my first IRL (in real life) time meeting a man on the dating app Hinge. Let's just say my experience led to my nearly coming un-hinged.

I pull my little black Honda Fit off the highway and into a parking lot. I'm wearing something pretty cute actually, because I'd dressed for the drink we were planning to have. About an hour before drink time, Parachute Boy texted to say, "Wanna meet at The Chief instead?"
Siy'ám' Smánit (The Stawamus Chief) is a stunning granite monolith, one of North America's largest and sacred to the Sḵwx̱wú7mesh (Squamish) Nation. This mountain now draws

outdoor enthusiasts from around the world to enjoy the short summer season living in their vans, walking slacklines in their yoga pants, and eating leftovers. Today the site draws adventure-seekers of all ilk, those who would climb—the hikers, climbers, mountaineers, and high-liners (who literally walk tightropes from peak to peak!), and those who would jump off—these being the paragliders and base jumpers. They come soaring in like flies to honey, the second the winter rains stop.

Moments after I park, a huge rusted out truck rolls in and a short-ish man leaps out (he literally has to jump down to the ground). I insert this rudely sexist observation because my date's online profile said something about him being 5'8 and there's no way he's 5'8. I can't blame him for stretching the truth—and will instead rightly blame our patriarchal conditioning, which is also responsible for women feeling overweight or too old or for sharing pictures from a few too many years ago. I know it's the person I'm here to meet though, because he's got the same man bun, as in his pics, and he's walking towards me. With my curly red hair, I tend to stand out in a crowd, which also makes it easy for my online dates to find me.

I begin to stroll towards him, smiling. I notice his blue eyes and his red backpack. We begin to hike the trail together, and I learn quickly that he's a logger. I'm a wilderness therapist and environmental activist, turned on in the 90s by the logging blockades in defence of the old growth forests of Clayoquot Sound. He's recently returned from cutting old growth, right around that same area. It seems we may have some incompatible values, yet I persist.

It's hard to say why I'm even on this date in the first place, but if I'm honest, it's because he asked me out and nobody's done that in a while. I'm also trying to move on from a lovely man I've been stuck on for the past year. You know how the saying goes: The best way to get over one man is to get under another.

What's much harder to determine than why I went on the date is why I stayed there once I learned what was in the enormous red backpack he wore. I've never been good at playing it cool, so I always ask early on: Do you want to have kids? (just kidding, that was my last date).

This time I say, "So, what's with the huge backpack?"

"Oh, it's my wing," he says, "I never hike The Chief without it."

It's a thing in this town. Depending on wind conditions, people like to hike up this huge rock, jump off the top and fly down. To do so, they carry up a sort of parachute called a wing—which, for the record, is not my thing.
The temperature suddenly drops and I'm freezing.

Before I proceed and for this to make sense to the lay person not living in Squamish, British Columbia, or what we call the Sea to Sky Corridor connecting Whistler on one end to Vancouver on the other, I need to explain that I live in the kind of gorgeously "epic" small coastal mountain town that draws in a lot of folks who self-medicate with adrenaline. There are days when I could have been counted in that number. It becomes quite clear early on that this is the case with this man, who has self-identified as such, both by way of his wing and by letting me know 5 minutes in that he is 37 years old and lives in his van (this in response to his questions to me: How old are you? And, do you own a house?).

When I learn of the parachute in his backpack, I pursue my line of questioning a moment longer.
"So...like...do you plan to use it?"
"Depending on the conditions!"

I should have bolted to my car at that point, but instead I quipped, "The conditions of the date?"

"No, the wind conditions," he stated, looking at me like I was totally missing the plot.

"Oh. And I guess I'd just walk down in the dark on my own then." I stated, more than asked.

At this point, my mind began inventing titles for this essay: "Peter Pan Really Does Think He Can Fly!" or "Over Before It Even Began" but again, for whatever reason I carried on up the mountain. At this point, I can only assume it was inertia, and not only just because I was already there, but because I'd done the same thing so many times before.

We did have some interesting conversations about the beautiful sorts of trees that I love and that he cuts down (we both love the humble Hemlock), and he was kind enough to carry a cold beer up to the top for me (a PBR, in case you're wondering). In the end, conditions were not right (both with the wind and the date) and so we walked back down together. At the parking lot, we went quickly to our separate vehicles and never spoke again.

Two days later when I was out running with my girlfriends I shook my head, disbelieving, as I shared the story.

"Oh wait, what's his name?" one of them asked after I finished telling them about the man who wore his escape route on his back on our first date.

When I shared his name, my friend raised her eyebrows.

"Wow! That's the guy Sarah's dating. They're heading away on a romantic weekend tonight."

A week later, during a cathartic conversation I shared the story with yet another friend. He looked back at me, shocked. His roommate had experienced the exact same thing, *with the exact same guy!* The only difference being that in her case the man actually did leap off the top of The Chief on the first date, and she chose to date him for three months thereafter. I suppose in their case conditions were right at first, though they broke up in short order when she learned he'd been secretly seeing another woman the entire time.

I can't judge the man too harshly though because I've been guilty of the same thing for much of my life. I used to rail against the boredom of mortgages, marriage and children but now it seems that's what I really want; not to trade in my wings for roots, but to find the balance of both. I mean I would prefer if he had been honest from the outset (even more explicitly honest about his unavailability than showing up wearing a parachute) but he wasn't the only one.

The 50-year-old man who invited me to dinner at his house this summer left our date up in the air (pun intended) as he waited to determine the wind conditions.
"Could I make you dinner Tuesday or Wednesday?" he asked me at the coffee shop.
It sounded like a lovely offer.

"Wednesday would be great!" I said.

"No, Tuesday *or* Wednesday," he repeated, like I hadn't heard him. "It depends on the wind." (The man wanted to go kiteboarding on whichever day should prove windier, keeping his options open so we could meet up on the latter day. It was clear where his priorities lay.)

Looking at it now, I really wonder why I went to the door anyway, but again, it had been a long time since I'd been asked on a date, and the offer of dinner was appealing. On the lower-wind-day he met me at the door of his home.
"Great to see you, your home is gorgeous!" I said.

"Thanks. It cost me 2.6 million dollars."

For ease, I'll refer to him as Blowhard.

There never was a second date.

Analytic psychologist Carl Jung explored the idea of adults whose emotional lives have remained at an adolescent level. In pop-psychology his idea of these folks who "won't grow up" has been referred to rather unkindly as *Peter Pan Syndrome*. On the surface there's the semblance of an immature character seeking joy and play, dodging responsibility, and commitment. I know I've presented this way to many suitors in the past. Jung notes two poles to this character: The positive side being the Child-God full of newness, potential for growth, and hope for the future, foreshadowing the hero he may become.

I have fallen for this potential over and over, and over again; drawn to the hopeful, fun, new childlike one with the potential to become the hero. I, myself, have been stuck right there with him, because I didn't yet know that I still needed to pass through my own portal of emotional puberty to cross the threshold to conscious, or evolved, adulthood. The negative pole of the "Peter Pan" concept is the resistance or refusal to grow up and meet the challenges of life face on, tending instead to blame others or lament circumstance as you sit waiting for your ship to come in and solve all your problems.

Jung conceived of this archetype leading a "provisional life", afraid of being caught in a situation from which it might not be possible to escape. The character covets independence and freedom, opposes boundaries, and limits, and tends to find any restriction intolerable. This fear of true intimacy and commitment (often a result of relational trauma) can lead to relating in ways that we therapists often refer to as enmeshment, or somewhat less kindly, codependency. I too have been trapped by the fear of making one of two seemingly irreparable mistakes: choosing the wrong person or missing the right one. These polarising fears keep us stuck in a devastating game of tug-of-war. In my case, for years, I struggled with these issues around love, trust, intimacy and leaning into the kind of healthy relationships where I could feel safe enough to simply be me.

So, the point is Parachute Boy, I've been there. I get you. Actually, a few years ago in Switzerland, I was the one literally wearing the parachute, but that's another story.

Now I'm in a different place. I'm ready for someone who isn't afraid to meet me head-on, and who's ready to stick it out through at least the first date, regardless of the conditions—wind or otherwise. Because now I'm ready for the real thing and I'm no longer open to being an accessory to somebody else's adventure, nor expecting them to come along for the ride on mine. I apologise profoundly to anyone I've left feeling that way.

You know, Parachute Boy wasn't so different from Blowhard who waited for the wind to change, or Scott who told me after our first weekend that he wasn't emotionally available (that was the moment I wish I'd followed my cousin's advice to share that I was "vehicularly unavailable" when Scott asked me for a ride). My experience with those guys wasn't even that different from the loving Jonas who let me know on our second date that he didn't want the same things I did.

They all told me the truth from the beginning, but I wasn't listening. I was so set on stamping them into the shape of my soulmate that I couldn't hear what they were telling me. So, I stayed, even though they told me right at the outset where they were going—which was off the cliff (and without me). It took me a long time to learn to listen, but I'm getting there. With Scott it took three years, with Jonas it took eight months, with Blowhard it was just the one dinner and with Parachute Boy it was two hours.

The next step is to just turn around and walk back to my car—which is what people who really love me always suggest when I tell them this story.

I'd like to thank you, Parachute Boy, for showing your cards so quickly. I appreciate you not pretending to be anything other than who you are (that's one I've done altogether too much). You saved me a lot of time, and besides, you've provided me with some excellent material here. I do hope you find the woman you're looking for, with a home of her own, but I also recommend you park your van and build one for yourself.

What I've learned about all this could fill a book (or maybe it already has). I used to think that keeping my running shoes by the door kept me free. Now I know that always keeping my eye to the exits was more about fear than anything else. What I thought was freedom was really my safety strategy. Now that I feel safe enough to be myself, now that I belong back to me, I see that we only need an escape route when we aren't already free.

So, so long Parachute Boy. May you land on your feet!

Will the Real Terry Please Stand Up

Dietmar Heine

40 years ago, I was feeling lonely, and wanted to meet some people for dates. Before online dating, the only way to message people was by putting an ad in a local paper and waiting for a response. I used NOW magazine, a weekly Toronto newspaper that had a gay personals section in the back. I recall the ad cost me $5.00.

WANTED...

Are you a man who's interested in dating a bright, creative, fun, and athletic university graduate? Do you aspire to share travel, movies, and other fun adventures? Would cooking supper together and having a quiet evening, talking together for hours on end appeal to you? I have been described as attractive, having a great sense of humour and being an old soul in an attractive young man's body. I'm tall, blond and love to laugh. If you're similar and interested in getting together for a chat over coffee, or a walk, please let me know. Thanks for your interest!

At the bottom of each personal ad was a unique code and no other contact information. If someone was interested in contacting you, they had to write a letter addressed to NOW magazine and place your unique code in a second sealed envelope. Once a week, NOW would send you a collection of letters from potential suitors.

A week after I placed my ad, I received a huge envelope that contained over 25 letters! Some of the letters were very short and contained simple sexual fantasies. Others were long, running to multiple pages. Topics included many personal details, including one person's entire life story! I eagerly read each letter and selected three of the most promising.

The letter that excited me most was written by a man named Terry, in beautiful cursive writing. On paper, Terry was articulate and funny and even though he hadn't included a picture of himself as most of the others had, Terry's sense of humour immediately got my attention. I decided to call him on the telephone first.

Our conversation lasted over an hour, as we laughed and shared some of our hopes, dreams, and funny dating stories. At one point, he described himself as passionate about arts, culture, and as someone who enjoys playing a variety of team sports. He told me he had blond hair, was over 6 feet tall, athletic, muscular, and tanned. He also added, "my friends and my mother tell me I am a catch!" When I asked Terry how old he was, he replied, "I'm in my early 30s." I was in my early 20s at the time, so the age difference didn't feel too big. After this fun conversation, both of us wanted to meet in person.

A few days after our first conversation, we had a second, much longer talk. We wanted to flirt a little more, and to pin down the location of our first date. I was even more excited, curious, and eager after that two-hour call. After four long days, we finally got to meet. The location was a downtown Toronto restaurant, on Yonge Street. Of course, I made sure that I had a fresh haircut, wore flattering clothing, flossed, gargled with mouthwash, and repeatedly brushed my teeth. I looked my best. My roommate said I looked hot as I was heading out.

Terry and I had agreed to meet for dinner at six o'clock. I was eager and arrived 25 minutes early. I wanted to make sure everything was just right. When I walked into the restaurant, there were three or four couples sitting at various scattered tables. I also noticed an older, bald man on his own, reading a newspaper near the front window. All the other tables were empty. I remember spending several minutes selecting just the right table; I wanted it to be as private as possible. I remember my hands sweating, and I felt quite flushed. I was completely excited about this new adventure!

I had brought a book with me while I was waiting, because I knew I was going to be early. I was so nervous, the words seemed invisible. A couple of minutes before six, I made a point of appearing extra nonchalant, and straightened my posture. I switched back-and-forth between the two chairs at the table at least three times, because I wanted my date to see me in the most flattering light.

Two more couples arrived and took tables nearby. As six finally arrived, I stopped pretending to read, and eagerly started scanning the front door of the restaurant. I strained my eyes, staring out through the large plate glass windows. 6:10 came and went, no Terry. At 6:20, still no Terry. I was beginning to get nervous and concerned. I wondered if Terry had been in some sort of accident, or worse, maybe he was standing me up.

At 6:25, the older man at the opposite side of the restaurant got up from his table, nervously wiped his glasses, and started towards me. He arrived at my table and said, "hello. Wow, you're even more attractive up close."

"Awww... thanks." I said.

"Sorry, I know I should have come over earlier and introduced myself," he said in almost a whisper.

I paused and looked at him. He spoke a bit louder and said, "I enjoyed watching you especially when you kept getting up and switching chairs. May I sit down?"
Confused and surprised, and thinking what's going on here? I stammered, "NO!"

In a flustered way, he said, "I'm so sorry for being late." He continued to stare at me because I was silent. He repeated himself, "May I sit down?"

I was confused. This man was in his mid-40s, bald, overweight, and certainly no taller than 5'7. I looked at him and said, "I'm sorry, but I'm waiting for a friend to show up."\

"Are you Dietmar?"

I was now even more confused, noting the way he was blushing as he spoke to me.
"How do you know my name?"
"I'm Terry. I wrote to you, and we had two phone conversations."

What the fuck!? I was shocked! Terry sat down at the table, even though I hadn't given him permission to join me. As he settled into his chair, I realized he had seriously exaggerated his age and physical attributes. I'm using the word exaggerated politely because the truth was that he had flat out lied to me.

Terry and I look at each other in silence for a few long seconds.

"I'm sorry for being late and for not coming over to talk to you when you first arrived," he said. "But you're so handsome—I was intimidated and too shy to approach you."

As he says this, I find myself becoming angry and sad. How is it possible for someone to lie so dramatically and not expect consequences?

At that moment, our waiter came over—I waved him away, "Give us a few minutes please."

I continued to stare at Terry. My anger was just below the boiling point. I don't like it when people lie to me. If Terry's description and age had been anywhere close to the person sitting across from me, all would have been forgiven. But in this situation, that was simply not possible. Not one thing he had told me about his physical appearance, or his age was true. Terry continued chatting away, as if he didn't have a care in the world. I continued to sit there and stare. I'm not even listening. I finally found my voice and interrupted his monologue.

"You lied to me about your age and your looks."

"I know. And I'm sorry," he said. "I was tired of constantly being rejected. When I saw your picture, I knew someone as handsome as you would never go on a date with someone who looks like me. I just wanted a chance."

"You have no idea who I am, what attracts me, or what my thoughts and feelings are about men. It's incredibly unfair of you to put me in this situation."

"But you wouldn't have dated me if you knew what I look like."

"I won't date you—ever!" I said. "Not because of the way you look or your age, but because you lied to me about those things. You've put such doubt in my mind. I wonder if anything you told me in our conversations is true. I'm so angry!"

I stood up and looked him right in the eye, "I'm walking out now because you lied, and I can't start anything with a liar."

As I started to walk away, Terry asked mournfully, "Do my looks matter to you?"

"Your looks don't matter at all right now, because I can't see you. I can't get past the lies."

With that, I left the restaurant feeling sad, angry, and upset. I couldn't believe that someone had so blatantly lied to me, just to get me to go on a date with him. I was also feeling a bit of shame because I suddenly realized that looks do matter to me—I had been lying to myself. Terry had been right. I would never date someone that looked like him.

awfully hilarious

Sophie Balisky

Chicago

I flew across Great Lakes to you
Separate skylines merged, I knew
That the light-blue calm of your embrace
Would give wings to words
And the fluttering of our hearts
Would unfurl one another free
From the chrysalis of us
Contained within possibility.

Fingertips trace faded scars
Like a connect the dots constellation
Of how our paths would someday cross
Under skyscrapers that glow like towers of stars

When wishing on one
Is to gaze up at them all...
Luminous dusk of the city
Lands upon our lips
As we catch feelings in open hands
With butterfly kisses and reckless abandon.

I am not a Diva

Bridget Fraser

So, here we were, I was leaning up against the shower wall, while my boyfriend was up to his wrist inside me, and neither of us were having a good time.

Let me introduce myself: I identify as an environmentalist, first and foremost. I studied ecology in college, and prior to her Green party leadership, Elizabeth May interviewed me to intern for the Sierra Club and live in her Ottawa basement. I teach outdoor environmental education and I wrote a master's thesis on what it means to be connected to nature. I am a greenie, a tree hugger, and an enthusiastic conservationist.

Since becoming an adult, I've made my living outdoors. And, as a person who menstruates, I've had my fair share of bloody messes.

Overnight leakage through your wool long johns —seeping into your down sleeping bag? Yup. Surprise period on a week-long backpacking trip without any supplies and forced to use your extra pair of wool socks instead of a pad? Been there. Sea kayaking trip off the coast with 20 teens trying to stay focused and present while the rain is pouring down, the wind is blowing hard, the students are hangry, and all you can think about is your very full tampon? Girl, I've got you.

Of course, there are many ways to deal with the hassles of having one's period in the backcountry. One of my colleagues would consume oral contraceptives throughout the month, to completely avoid having their period. To some this may seem unnatural and maybe even unhealthy, but as some doctors like to point out, women of previous eras were usually either pregnant or breast-feeding for much of their lives and actually had far fewer periods than we do today. Perhaps some folks see the pill as a reasonable option and are ok with trading monthly bleeding for some disconnect with their cycle, but for me it's not a compelling argument.

For those of us for whom the daily pill is not an option, we take on the euphemistically named feminine hygiene products, a.k.a. the plug and the mattress-between-the-legs. These products present a number of logistical challenges: first, find the time to escape; tag out with your female colleague—You're in!

Bring the bag of goodies, hidden in your jacket—the bag of unused items (hopefully still dry and intact), the wet-wipes, the hand sani, the toilet paper, and the bag to contain the whole bloody mess. Hot tip: dog poop bags are ideal. Find semi-private location and avoid bleeding on your week's supply of clothes as you juggle to keep items dry in the rain, while looking over your shoulder for bears and students.

And then, the biggest challenge: where to keep your bloodied items? We are warned that bears can smell anything—ANYTHING! For god's sake, keep your granola wrappers and lip balms out of your tent, for it will attract every bear west of the Rockies. Your bloody tampons and pads must be kept safe, in a bear cache. But apparently if you're bleeding throughout the night, you're totally fine? Menstrual blood doesn't smell like food, so don't worry about it. WHAAT?? We continue to pretend to believe this ridiculous thinking, for what? So, we can ease our minds? Because, what's the alternative? Not camping for 25% of our adult life? Not fucking likely.

When it comes to tampons, less is more, right? The green alternative is to have no applicator at all, but when you're looking at your filthy, ragged fingernails (youch!) that haven't seen soap in a week, do you really want to violate your beautiful yoni with that bacterial mess? HELL no, sister! You know you'll end up with more issues than just bloodied clothes. Also, when our bodies get cold, all our warm blood heads to the uterus—even when it's vacant—which leaves my tampon-inserting digits frozen, floppy, and frustratingly useless. Even if I was able to push the cotton high enough, I cringe at the added potential for a bloody batch of yeasty goodness with a cherry-on-top trip to an ER. It's a nightmare waiting to happen!
Which brings me to why I chose to try the Diva cup. It checked all the boxes: it's reusable and

eliminates days of packing wet, heavy bear-attractants. It seemed simple enough: insert, bleed, release. Except, there I was, my first time using it, in a public restroom stall, with my right hand covered in blood, trying to grasp the slippery, rubbery nub of the end of my Diva. Despite my best yogic contortions and rock-climber clawing, I could not release the cup. Blood dripped onto my clothes and onto the restroom floor, panic rising as I considered the possibilities: toxic shock syndrome, a trip to the emergency room, or worse yet, the public humiliation of a blood tsunami as my cup overfloweth. It was at this moment, that I suddenly recalled, an awkward conversation with a physician, several years ago, who gave me an exam (an older, white, male physician, I should add).

“Has anyone ever told you that you have a very long vagina?” He asked.

I remember being speechless. How the fuck was I, or anyone, supposed to respond to that question?

“Yes, thank you!”

"No... but that explains a lot."
"Has anyone ever suggested that you might have some envy?"
"Your description might say a lot more about you than it does about me, my friend."

Despite my rising anxiety, I got through the day, and as soon as my boyfriend got home, I explained the situation.

And, so here we are, back at the beginning, naked in the bathroom, me wedged in the corner of the tub, with one foot jammed on the rim, grabbing onto the top of the shower. Him donning a headlamp, on his knees, fishing around inside me, trying to grab onto the Diva while I breathe through the pain.
He stops, "I don't think I can do this— it just feels wrong. I'm obviously hurting you— you're bleeding everywhere!"

I urge him to press on. Finally, he releases the cup's suction, and its contents splash across the tub. Sweet Jesus! It looks like a CSI scene.

Hours later, after I'd had a chance to recover emotionally, I suggested alternatives that I might be able to try to avoid this in the future, "maybe we could clove-hitch a long piece of dental floss to the bottom of the Diva, like a tampon string?"

He just looked at me. We both knew that emotionally we could not do this again—our relationship would not survive another Diva disaster. I tossed out the cup and unwrapped a plug. Which is how I came to realize, I am not a Diva.

awfully hilarious

The One Where Our Girlfriends Save the Day

Paris

This is the story of a great date. But not for the reasons you might expect.

To set the scene, it's a few months into the COVID-19 pandemic. There is no vaccine yet, and we're constantly weighing the risks and benefits of every social interaction.

I notice I'm getting much choosier about who I'll meet for a first date—if I'm going to risk getting this super contagious unpredictable virus it's not going to be for just anyone. But Kyle seems like a super sweet and genuine guy, and we've already had some deeper than usual conversations before we meet in person.

Our first date is the standard pandemic times meet-up: coffee and a walk. It's pleasant, perhaps not scintillating, but these are such awkward times it takes more than one interaction to write someone off completely. First dates are awkward enough to begin with, then add in the extra layers of, do we hug? Do we touch? Do we try to maintain a six-foot distance between us at all times? It's a lot to navigate on a first date. So while it doesn't feel like a total click, I feel into him enough that I want to meet up again.

It's coming on winter, so for our second date he suggests a local brewery that has winterized their outdoor patio with big cozy fires and lots of blankets. I appreciate the extra care that they've put into keeping us all toasty as we try to keep ourselves safe and sane. I wrap up warm in all the layers and blankets and sit at a rustic table by a blazing fire while I wait for Kyle. I picked this table because I noticed two women, my age, enjoying themselves on the other side of the fire. They've got a sparkle to them, that energetic thing that happens when women get together to tell stories and have a laugh. I feel a pang of longing thinking about my own girlfriends and how often we've done the same thing. This pandemic has made the rare times we can safely gather with friends all the more precious. I smile at them, and they beam back, putting me at ease as I glance down at the menu.

When Kyle arrives, I sense that something is wrong right away. He seems to be shifting around a lot, avoiding eye contact, and unable to find a comfortable position to sit in on our bench. He orders a kombucha and tells me he can't drink tonight. He was at a bachelor party two days ago and he overdid it. He thinks his liver isn't back to optimal functioning yet. "Optimal functioning." These are his actual words. I turn it into a joke, thinking we can laugh about it and move on. And for a while we do. Within a few minutes we're back into the deep stuff again as the conversation turns towards spirituality, karma, and the afterlife—y'know, second date stuff.

Half an hour goes by and suddenly he seems to be withdrawing from the conversation, trying to wrap things up. I notice he also seems to be slumping further and further back on the table behind his bench. Is it just COVID cautiousness, I wonder? Is the smoke from the fire getting in his eyes? Did I eat something with onions in it for lunch?

I'm wondering if I should say something and ask him what's going on, when he gets out his phone and shoots off some rapid texts. His phone quickly gets a buzz in response.

"My friend is going to come pick me up," he says abruptly. "I need to go to my naturopath and get something for my liver. I'm worried it's getting worse."

I nod my understanding, even though I don't entirely understand. Why did he come on the date if he was feeling this unwell, I think to myself? How is his naturopath open at 7pm on a Thursday night, I ponder further? He excuses himself to use the restroom and 10 minutes later he's back and waving for the bill at the same time as his friend conveniently pulls up in some loud white sports car across the street. I still have half my drink left.

"I hope you feel better soon. I'm just going to stay and finish this," I say.

Clutching his side and practically doubled over, he hobbles away and gets into the white sports car. Seconds later the car is peeling away from the curb and Kyle is never to be seen or heard from, by me, again.

As soon as his car door slams shut, I notice one of the women across the fire trying to catch my eye. I give her a wan smile and she immediately leans forward around the flames and asks, "Um, were you just on a date and did he just leave?" Her voice is shrill and ringing with incredulity on the words 'date' and 'leave.'

"It was a date. And yes, he just left. He said he thought his liver was shutting down."
Reva and Clare are instantly equal parts outraged and amused on my behalf.

"Did he at least pay for your drink?"

I reassure them that he did.

"Well, we're buying you another one."

We instantly bond over my re-telling of the whole story from start to finish, and spend the next two hours drinking beers, eating pizza, and crying with laughter as we exchange online dating horror stories around the fire. There's the one about the guy Reva dated for six months before finding out about his long-term relationship with someone else. And Clare's story about the girl who got arrested for caking the handles of her ex's car in dog shit. Dog shit leads to my story about the guy who brought his giant dog on our first date and didn't pick up its giant sidewalk shits.

It feels ancient and cathartic. A group of women sharing their stories of the ones who have ghosted us or the ones who we've ghosted when things have gone in a direction that we didn't like. Sharing in the calamity, the hilarity, and the resilience of navigating dating and relationships. I think about how many women have gathered around a fire and done just this all around the world, across cultures and time—since time immemorial. It feels like sisterhood. It feels like our ancestors are here at our backs, hands on our shoulders, as they laugh along with us. I tell the girls that this unexpected time with them has been the best outcome from a date that I've had in a long while.

We take the final sips of our drinks, and feeling settled in our souls, we decide to settle the bill and head out into the night. It's a gorgeous winter evening and as soft flakes start falling from the darkened sky, Reva and Clare offer to walk me home.

And it's then that I realize the beauty of sharing these experiences with one another, with you, with our sisters and friends. The healing of being able to laugh about these things together—we are reaching out a hand, leaning across the fire, and reassuring each other: It's alright, I see you, I hear you, I've got you. Let's talk about it. It'll make it easier. I promise.

In the end we really are all in this together. In the words of Ram Dass, "we are all just walking each other home."

Gratitude

First, thank you to all the contributors. Your brave voices and your stories matter. Holding hands with you has been such an honour (and has made all the painful parts a whole lot more palatable). It's been a blessing to both dance, and to disrupt with you.

Thank you to our families, our partners, our lovers, our Tinder matches, our lonely nights, our terrible first dates, and most of all to our pals, without whom none of these stories would have ever become funny, nor seen the light of day.

Thank you, Earth, Sun and Moon, who have held and nurtured us always, and whose cycles we followed as we wove these pages, transforming our painful moments through love, inclusive sisterhood, and belonging, in beloved community.

Thanks to april joseph, for coaching this project to completion, for holding my hand, and for her constant and gentle guiding light. Thank you to Linds & to Paris, and to all my sisters, for conceiving of this project in the first place, for laughing right away, and for always coming out to dance with me in the moonlight.

Thank you to June Lucarotti and the Birth Your Book writing community, because community is everything (am I right?!)

Thank you to Meg Power, our editor, who offered support and feedback to help our contributors put their best story forward. Thank you so much to our first readers, Anne and Pam, who laughed in all the right places, and who helped to midwife and make this work ready for the world.

Thank you to designer Ken Braithwaite, whose generosity, eye for detail, and ability to implement and produce this book have helped so many of my ideas become real.

Thank you always to Gerardo Marquez for holding fast to the light, and for creating a container for all contributors to safely gather, share and propel this project to higher heights.

In closing, thank you dear reader. We're doing this work of transformation, transmutation, growth, and healing through storytelling with you, for you, and alongside you. You being here means everything. Our hope is that these words reach you at a time when you need them.
You belong here.

Til next time!

Love,
Heather

p.s. Want to contribute a story to the series? Send your most awfully hilarious, transmuted "taboo" moments to us at:

www.awfullyhilarious.com

Can't wait to hear from you!

Made in United States
North Haven, CT
25 January 2023

31637670R00112